FISHING ROPES

Tales from the Retired Fisherman

– TREVOR J POTTER –

This book is a collection of tales from the men that worked the ropes. In the UK it was all trawling, until the Second World War, then the Danish fishermen came over. Anchor fishing and fly shooting was then started by the British fishermen. Also it was more of a family business. Not run by the big trawler owners.

I hope you enjoy reading their story's as much as I did, putting them on paper.

An environmentally friendly book printed and bound in England by
www.printondemand-worldwide.com

This book is made entirely of chain-of-custody materials

www.fast-print.net/store.php

Fishing with the Ropes – Tales from the Retired Fisherman
Copyright © Trevor J Potter 2012

All rights reserved

No part of this book may be reproduced in any form by photocopying or any electronic or mechanical means, including information storage or retrieval systems, without permission in writing from both the copyright owner and the publisher of the book.

ISBN 978-178035-516-0

First published 2012 by
FASTPRINT PUBLISHING
Peterborough, England.

Contents

Chapter 1 - The Ropes.   3
Chapter 2 - Ronny Jenson.   9
Chapter 3 - Arie Van-Zandvliet.   15
Chapter 4 - My Tales.   21
Chapter 5 - The Dangers.   26
Chapter 6 - The Skippers.   32
Chapter 7 - James Purdy Cullen.   40
Chapter 8 - Terry Fairley.   45
Chapter 9 - Ray Morse.   51
Chapter 10 - The Crew.   56
Chapter 11 - Egon Thomson.   68
Chapter 12 - Allsorts.   78
Chapter 13 - Cliff Ellis.   83
Chapter 14 - Back To The Lads   88
The End Of Fishing. Pete Fryer Let Go   93

With Thanks.

I would like to thank all the men that shared their lives with me, not only the ones that the chapters are named after, but all the other guys that backed up the story's. The men who sailed with them, I would also like to thank Peter Fryer for allowing me to use his photo collection. LET GO. Amber online.com.

My wife Pat Peach Potter, not only for the spelling but she told me when to explain things to the layman.

This book is dedicated to all fishermen of all nations. Certainly to the Danish fishermen who gave us the ropes.

Last But Not Least. My Late Mother.

She will never be forgotten, as long as there are trawlers fishing for prawns in the Farne deeps. As that is where she lays.

Chapter 1 - The Ropes

This book is a collection of stories that I have put together, from the men I have sailed with, and fished against, hopefully you will enjoy their stories a much as I did talking to them, and learning a lot. I have been through a lot of books written by ex fishermen, but most were about trawling. This one is about anchor bashing, Danish anchor seine netting. This type of fishing first came to the UK during the Second World War, as a lot of Danish fishermen, to save their boats, sailed to Fleetwood.

From then on during the war years fished the Irish Sea in the winter months, and the coast of Iceland in the summer. After the war most of them stayed in the UK, but moved to the east coast ports as this type of fishing was better suited to the shoal water, of the North Sea. This is why, if you ever go to Grimsby, you will find that a lot of the locals have Danish names. Also Whitehaven was a popular port for some of the Danish fishermen, a lot of the lads I got to know were born there.

Also all of the anchor boats were family owned, not like the big trawler firms in the UK. The boats were built from wood, not steel and the crew, four at the most, were on a share, no wages at all, so if they caught nothing, they got nothing. As simple, or hard as that. But when they did make a big trip, their money was treble, compared to a trawler deck hand. Before I get into the yarns I will explain the working of an anchor boat, how it catches fish, and why it was kind to the seabed.

Trawling is very hard on the seabed, especially the soft ground trawlers, as they towed a lot of chain in front of the net, to dig out the flatfish, and that killed a lot of the feed, e.g. worms, small shellfish, and the eggs of the fish that were laid just under the sand.

Where as an anchor boat used no chain and only the ropes that were shot, (three mile of them) skimmed over the bottom and made a cloud of sand that the fish would not swim through. Also the tide was a big factor, if the gear of an anchor boat was not hauled against the tide then the ropes would not dig, and so no fish, but a trawler could tow her net in any state of the tide, and in any direction and still catch fish.

The horse power of a trawler determined on the amount of fish caught. The bigger the engine, the bigger the chance of good fishing. Where as It did not matter if an anchor boat had 100 HP, or 1000 HP, it was the ropes that caught the fish. And without a very good anchor, one that held the seabed well, then you were wasting you're time. Here Is a diagram of the anchor gear, first off it was at least a quarter of a mile long, starting with the anchor then a very heavy chain, then 30 fathom of wire, (60 meters) then another 10 meters of chain, that acted as a spring, after that was another 90 fathom of wire, one very large float, and another 30 fathom, then another float, then to finish off, yet another 30 fathom of wire to the boat.

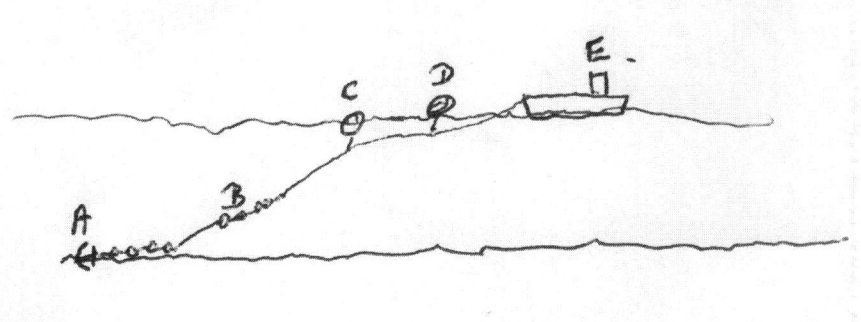

Sorry about the diagram but I am no artist, my wife said I am, but I think she means a piss artist. Anyway you get the idea of anchors rig up.

A = admiralty type anchor

B = spring chain, this lifts and drops to help take the strain off the anchor.

C = first float, about three meters round, this does two jobs, 1 to hold the gear up, 2 it acts as another spring.

D = second float, this one is to hold the gear on the surface, also a standby in case the other one bursts, or is lost.

E = Trevor in the wheelhouse, praying this all works.

On the next note I will try to explain how the fishing gear works, first at the anchor, then fly shooting, as in Scotland, with the tides being so slack, they found this mode of using the ropes worked better.

The tide in the North Sea runs in different directions, depending on what part you are in, near the coast of England it runs NNW for 6 hours then SSE for another six. In mid North Sea it runs NE and SW, hope you know the compass ?. when you get to the south of the North Sea it runs east and west. Some skippers used a tide indicator (bit of rag on a line,) but I was told, always go by the book, e.g. tide times on the chart and I did find that it was the best way, not often mother nature gets it wrong. Lets say mid summer that has the longest daylight hour's some skippers will try for five hauls per day, and others six.

I found after a few years that less hauls, on the tide, was better than more hauls, with some of them across the tide. Am I getting boring yet well here is another of my master drawings, to help you understand that bit.

This pic shows how the gear would be shot on the seabed. Note the dotted haul, this would be shot on the turn of the tide, it was not often that this gave the same reward. Some skippers never bothered with this and so moved the anchor. While other skippers shoot up to six hauls on the same anchor spot. Each to their own, me being a bit of a lazy bugger I stuck to the long slow hauls.

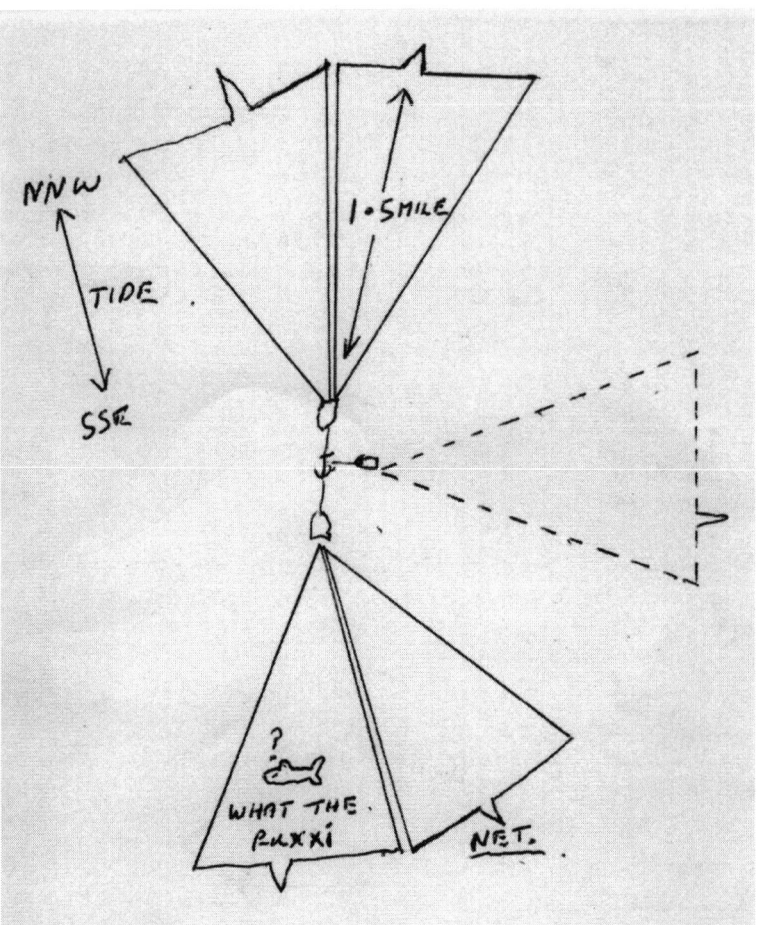

Also during the early years, there were a lot of Danish boats from Fredrikshaven fishing with ropes in the Moray Firth and this got the local boats very interested, as they were mostly herring drifters, and small trawlers, so this is how the ropes started in Scotland, or so I am told, and who am I to argue with the older men.

From then on fly shooting was born. The difference between the two types of rope fishing, one the south side ports used the anchor, where as the northerly ports used the propeller to hold the gear tight. The middle ports (North Shields) used both methods, lucky buggers.

The advantage that the fly shooters had, they could fish on harder ground, also steam about picking off the best bits of ground, if they saw fish marks on the echo sounder, then they shot the ropes around them, after that haul they would be away looking for more marks. The big disadvantage was the fuel that they had to burn, for example one day I was talking to the skipper of the Lindisfarne, Jimmy Bailey, we had both done a ten day trip. And both had around 250 boxes of fish, his were cod and haddock, mine were flatfish. Well he asked me how much fuel I had used, it was 200 gallons, and his boat had used 2000 gallons, wow that is amazing, but my boat used an anchor to catch fish, and anchors do not burn fuel. Do not get me wrong, over a year Jim would double my earnings, that made up for the fuel cost and the larger crew, but as the years passed, and the cost of fuel rising, the fly shooters were the first to go.

Well now you know as much as me, as far as fishing with ropes, I have called this book under the shadows, because that is how the small boats were regarded by the trawler owners, skippers, and sadly a lot of the deck crew. But as the years went on and the trawler fleet went tits up they then started to sail with us, and a lot of them changed their opinion.

In the trawler hey days the crews would use different pubs, but even they were separated, as the trawler skippers and mates would not mix with their own deck crew.

On the anchor boats, while in dock our skipper would mix with us, and have a lot more respect for us. I think because we had a small crew you just had to get on. Even silly things, like taking ice, the trawlers went first, and the anchor boats had to get their ice after. We could not complain as the big firms had shares in the ice factory, also they ran the engineering firms, the fuel pumps, and even the shops that sold us sea gear. And every one was charged 25p for every £1.00 they spent. As time went by the smaller boats would buy their gear and other things on the high street, but the trawlers were tied to the same shops, run by the big firms.

In the early to mid sixty's most of the trawler firms knew what was coming for the fleet, and started to build Anchor Boats, (from now on I will call them snibbys, as that was the nick name for them) but they kept them separate from the trawlers. For an instance Banisters trawlers had about six trawlers, all called Saxon whatever, ONWARD, FORWARD, but they had two Snibbys built, Saxon King and Saxon 11, Two, sorry I have not got a roman key board.

Any way the two Snibbys were not run by Banisters, they were put in the care of Arcona Fishing Co, they had about six other boats, bet you can not guess the first name of them? Yep Arcona Whatever, Bay,

Lad, and so on. I often wonder why they did that, but I am sure it was a money matter. In the mid 70s the trawler deck crews decided to strike, for better pay, so to stop this the owners got crews from other ports to crew the boats, now one small problem with this, as the strike breakers arrived at the boat, then all hell broke loose.

They then decided to take the trawler out in to the Humber River, drop anchor and let the snibbys (that they owned) ferry the new crews out to the awaiting trawler. Now this caused a lot of trouble around the town as the striking crews blamed all anchormen, but it was only the trawler owned snibbys that did this. So we all suffered, and the divide widened. But in 1974 when all the snibbys and small boats all over the UK decided to blockade the ports, to stop cheep frozen fish coming in on the ferries, it was a different story as not one large trawler backed us up and the only reason that it had to end was because the government said that our boats would be taken off us, with 70% of the boats family owned we were up (as they say in Germany) shiten straser. Well all, I now want to go onto tales from the retired fishermen, and by f**k it has opened my eyes. Some are funny some are sad, but if they are true or not, well you will have to ask them.

But I do believe the ones that told me. Also would a fisherman EVER tell a lie?

Chapter 2 - Ronny Jensen

I would like you all to meet Ron, it is funny that we sailed out of North Shields at the same time, but never became friendly until we retired, do not get me wrong, we never had a bad word for each other but it is a fact that some fishermen never mix. I think it was because I was a gabby sort of guy, where as Ron was more the quiet type, but always friendly.

On speaking to Ron and asking about his life at sea, I found that he had a bigger sense of humour than I gave him credit for sorry Ron. He told me that his father, Magnus Kampman Jensen, came over to England in 1937, as I said earlier the Danish men got out before the war. He settled in Whitehaven, and fished from there during the war years.

Ronny Jenson was born in 1945, in White haven, he started fishing at the age of 15, on a boat called the Neils Resager which was an anchor basher, in time he went mate on a boat called the Fairway, now he told me that I must mention this boat, as it was one of the best he sailed in. maybe because he made a lot of money, or the fact that he felt safe in her. I would like to think the latter.

Here is a picture of Ronny when he was mate on the Fairway. At 18

Ron Jenson, keeping the gear level, by feeling the tension on each rope, this was a very fine art, not only in feeling the tension, but knowing if one rope was dragging through a bit of hard ground. This he could tell by slacking on the tight rope if it did not get any slacker Ron then knew that it was hanging up on the seabed, there on he would go by the splices in the ropes to keep the net semi level, after the rope was clear he would then go back to bringing the gear home by feel and the eye.

As Mac in the coral Bank told me, not many men were good at this, as it took a lot of years practice, and a lot of common sense, note that in those days the rope was coiled onto the deck and had to be stacked ready for the next haul. Can you imagine three mile of rope being stacked away every haul, so five hauls in one day made 15 miles of rope to be dragged away and lifted.

With only two men doing this job, well you are knackered, but it did not end there as when the ropes were all in, you then had a net to pull in by hand, if you were cod fishing they floated, but if you were flat fishing it was a very heavy task. On top of that add a bag of sea weed or shells, god I must have been nuts. To be honest we all were.

Ron sat for his skippers ticket in 1967, not for himself but to allow his father to take a bigger boat, and this is to me a very bad thing as all the years that Magnus had been skipper, with no major hiccups the English law decided that he had to have a ticket man on the boat, this happened a lot in GY, Danish men even those with a skippers ticket could not take a boat to sea, the amazing thing is that the ticket that they did have allowed them to take a large vessel from Denmark, but not a small fishing boat from England, (how sad), so a lot of Danish men were called the fishing instructor, and an English lad with a ticket were the skipper. I call it a ticket, and not a certificate because to me some of the men that got one, ?? well put it this way I would not let them take my dog for a walk.

Anyway back to Ronny, he told me a very funny yarn that his father talked about, during the war years all crew members of fishing boats had to learn how to use a Lewis Machine Gun, that was fixed on to the forward part of the boat, to me it is a bit like pissing into the wind, if a sub or an aeroplane was attacking my boat the last thing I would do was upset them even more. Well we were only carrying fish, so is that worth fighting a U Boat for.

If they wanted a few haddock, well they only had to ask, and I would have given them the whole fish room full. Any way this lad had been for a mid day pint, and on his return had to cook a meal for the lads, in them days the only thing to cook on was a coal stove, no problem, light the fire and get stuck in, but when he opened the coal locker, (it was under the bench in the cabin) he found that the lumps of coal were to big, well to me that is a hammer job, but no he decided to do it the easy way, he opened the skylight went on deck and set up the Lewis gun, hey it worked great, after firing a few rounds into the coal and breaking all the big lumps up to fit the stove he then proceeded to cook the dinner so all was well ? except for one tiny detail, the bullets went through the hull and the boat sank. And on top of that the dinner was fu★★ed.

Skipping back to the Fairway, Ronny told me that one day as they were heaving in the ropes, the cook, a lad named Ronny Blacklock was stood beside him, stacking the forward ropes when the gear in the water started to act very strange, like one rope suddenly dipped very low in the water, then sprang back to normal, then the other rope lifted very high and sprang across the other neither of the lads had ever seen anything like it, then all of a sudden two very large black and white whales popped up and blew.

What a fright they both got, not the whales, the two lads, I know this is true as I have had the same happened to me, when the whales are playing with the ropes it is a very strange sight, also with them being the same or bigger length than the boat it was very scary when they decide to rub their backs on the hull, it's a case of hold tight and hope.

This could only happened to the two Ronny's. I bet you thought that I had missed that?.

As the years went on Magnus Jensen bought a boat from Denmark and based her in North Shields, she was called the Nette Oster, 60 foot long, 49 ton and16 foot beam. That is a large boat for her time so she warranted a skippers ticket luckily Ronny had his so he was the official skipper even though his dad was the fishing skipper, the first two years things did not go to well, being a suppositious man Magnus said it was because she had her name changed.

When she was launched she was called the Mimos!e so he changed her name back to the English name for that Mimosa, SN23, and after that they never looked back. I must mention one man here, Kaj Poul Sorensen, this man sailed with Magnus for 23years, and then did 7 years with Ronny, that is what I call a reliable crewman, Ron also had another lad with him Kevin Caffery, and he sailed on Mimosa for 7 years, so the job must have been ok. Kev went on to be a very successful skipper owner, and to this day still holds the port record for the biggest trip ever made in GY for an anchor boat. Sorry but I cannot tell you how much that was as he keeps breaking it. Going back to Ronny he took over command of Mimosa in 1970 when hid dad retired and kept up the good work, in the winter months while most of the GY fleet were laid up, the Mimosa would change over to trawling for prawns, and that boosted the yearly earnings.

Fishing with the Ropes

The Mimosa before her refit in mid 1980s she then had a whaleback fitted which made life a lot better for the lads on deck, a happy crew is a hard working crew.

I asked Ronny if at anytime in his career did he have a bad any bad experiences, it was a silly question as all fishermen did at some time or other. But one that stuck in his mind was when he almost lost the Mimosa.

He was laid at anchor, in a north easterly storm, about 160 miles NE of the Tyne, obviously he was not fishing but on inspecting the engine room he found a lot of water, his engine was running but for some reason the bilge pump was not.

After getting the lads on the hand pump, he then checked the main bilge pump, normally it is just the filter but he found that it had given up life as a pump, and decided it wanted to be a bit of scrap, I think that was very inconsiderate on the pumps behalf with it being bad weather at the time.

Next he parted the anchor gear, I have been through this and I can tell you it is not pleasant, well Ron decided to head for home, and for the whole trip of 160 miles the lads had to keep on the hand pump.

Luckily they kept the water at a safe level, but being in a storm with the wind behind you is not a nice thing. If he had taken a wave over the stern, well all I can say is that I would not be typing this chapter.

Well to end I would like to show a picture of Mimosa after the refit, and as you can see the crew were better protected from the weather.

what a big difference.

Thank you Ronny Jensen for your help.

Fishing with the Ropes

Chapter 3 - Arie Van-Zandvliet

Well where do we start with this man, born in Wallsend, North Shields, he started fishing from his home port, but Arie was not happy with the fact that he did not pay tax every trip, that may sound strange to you but he told me that he preferred the GY style of paying his tax every trip.

So 1962 he went to GY and started fishing on an anchor boat called the Brig, the skipper was an Old Danish man called Karl Rees. I remember this skipper well, as he was a drinking buddy of one of my x skippers, Jack Clark, (Canadian Jack) he was the skipper of a boat called Maxwell. Another snibby. Arie told me that Karl was a great man to sail with, very laid back sort of chap, he also said that it was his brain that caught the fish, and not luck. I said what do you mean not luck?.

Arie then went on to tell me about how UNLUCKY Karl was. He broke his leg at sea, not a clean break, it was a nasty one, so karl was in plaster for about six month, to be honest whenever I saw him he was plastered sorry could not help that little quip. Any way the day he got his plaster off, there he goes into the club, on Cleethorp Road to celebrate getting back to sea, on his way home he fell in the road and a taxi ran over his leg, shit another three month in plaster.

By the way I did not tell you that Arie is one of our coloured brethren maybe that is why he was called Black Harry. I did ask him if this ever made any impact on his early fishing days, he laughed and said only once,

A boat called the Clee was looking for a crewman, the skipper was a Danish lad Ina Eskersen but when he met Arie he said no, so the owner of the boat asked the skipper what the problem was, and was told that he did not like the look of him, any way Arie did sail with him and did two years on the Clee.

Now that should teach the whole world something, Arie did two years on the Clee, and also told me that it was the hardest boat he tried to leave. I never met Arie until later in my career but had been told a lot about him, mostly about what a very laid back guy he was, that is until you upset him, and then watch out. He told me that one day he went in the Dolphin bar on North Shields fish quay to have a pint with a skipper from Grimsby, Jimmy Howard this man had just got a share in the boat that he was skipper of, while he was chatting away Jim told him that he was sailing that evening, so did not want to drink too much, the mate a lad named Bob Mc Queen, who by the way was no light weight said that he was not sailing as he wanted another night in Shields.

Jim said that he was trying to make money for the crew not spend it, but bob was adamant that he was not sailing until the next day

Bang one hit off Arie and big Bob was on the deck, and he did not get up, any way the same evening Arie drove down to the quay, and the boat had sailed. I love that yarn, as Bob was known as a hard guy Arie was not.

Arie Van-Zandvliet this was taken in 2012. at a Scottish museum, note the big smile, imagine him in the 1960s.

Fishing with the Ropes

He sat for his skippers ticket in 1976 in South Shields, and told me that his first boat was out of his home port of North Shields, was an anchor boat called Vibek J Laj, he did not do well in her but how many skippers did in their first year, she was owned by a man called Joe Stevenson, he also owned a very famous boat called the Stranby.

Arie then decided to go back to Grimsby (GY), and in in 1980 he took command of the Ling Bank but he told me that he never really liked her as a sea boat.

I was shocked at this as I took her in 1973, (my first skippers job) and found her to be a great boat, but there was a big difference, as after I had her away she was given a big refit, new wheelhouse and whaleback, so this turned a good sea boat into a bad one he told me that he was laid in a storm, with the bad weather gear out when she hit a big wave, her nose went under and the decks filled with water.

All anchor boats were made to ride the wave, but with the whaleback being to heavy for her, it changed her into one of the bad ones.

She was built in Buckie, by herd and McKenzie and after a very successful fleet of boats that they did build, then maybe the owners of the boats should have had their refit in the same shipyard, it would have been safer as the men that built the boats would have known how to change them.

LING BANK

17

Note the length of her whaleback, (deck cover) it kept the crew dry, as in Mimosa, but this time it was too heavy, also she had a steel wheelhouse and this new one is fibreglass. So doubling the weight at the forward end, and half the weight aft, well that is asking for trouble, as most seamen would tell you.

After her Arie took a boat called the Saxon King, another one that I had been skipper of, do you think he is stalking me? Now this boat he did like, as I did she was a great sea boat, and built on the same plan as the Ling Bank, the difference was they left her as she was built, and that proves a lot.

When he took her over she was iced and ready for sea, as the last skipper, Tony Chester for some reason left while she was stored up and ready for a trip, Arie was not to keen on taking another mans boat as he preferred to stock up himself, but any way he did.

He then told me a yarn that made me smile. On the first day fishing the crew were a bit weary of Black Harry, as he was known in GY, and made a big fu** up when shooting the gear, so even though it was flat calm weather Arie told them to stop the job and make a breakfast.

So all sat in the cabin with the breccy on the table Arie said to the lads that all he wanted off them was to take their time, and get it right, not run around like blue arsed flies just to keep the skipper happy.

After that everything went great,

Saxon King, my favoured boat and Aries.

Fishing with the Ropes

He told me an amusing yarn, one day he was talking to Mac, Coral Bank, Mac said to him that he had made history, when Arie asked how Mac replied that there was now a black prince in command of a Saxon boat, if you do not get that one read up un your history

Another tale I was told about Arie, was off a long time shipmate of mine, Eifion Owen Elias, from now on Taffy, he told me that he had sailed with Arie on a boat called the Dover Star. At sea he was told to get two new coil of rope out of the engine room, now a coil of rope is 120 fathoms long, (250 meters), three stranded rope with a core of lead in each strand, now that is heavy, anyway Taff and the other lad were struggling with the rope, when Arie came aft put a rope through the coil, took a turn on the net hauler, in a flash the new rope was on the deck, as he walked away he said to Taffy, "do not use energy when there is machinery" and to me, not a truer word said.

In 1981 Arie bought a half share in the Saxon King, and renamed her Delvan, Delger fishing Co, and Van-zandvliet, I wish I had put my bid in for her instead of the Toledo.

But there you go, as I said earlier in the book, trawler firms often had Anchor boats built, but did not run them, Fred Bannister had the two Saxon boats, but one day he woke up dead, and so the two boats went up for sale, and both renamed, Saxon King became the Delvan, and Saxon11 was renamed the Peace wave.

She came to a sad end, one night while the crew were in their bunks she was hit by a merchant vessel, and went down with all hands. R.I.P.

On a lighter note Arie told me that he wanted to get new rope reels on Dover Star, and for the type he wanted you are talking £9000.00.

He had been told that a boat called the Grenna Pearl had been decommissioned , (no longer allowed to fish) was to become a museum boat for the fishing heritage in Hull, so off he goes and spoke to the heritage centre, Arie told them that it was not history, as in the old days anchor boats had to stack the ropes on the deck, after being coiled by a chain driven coiler.

After a long chat they asked him if he could help, and he did, there was a lot of old Beccles coilers laid in GY, so he told them that if they paid for the crane to lift the reels off, he would fit a coiler free of charge, and stack the ropes in the old fashioned way. They were over the moon.

Arie was even good enough to dispose of the old reels for them, free of charge.

Well they got their coiler, and Arie got new reels for the Dover Star

I love that story, good on you mate.

Chapter 4 - My Tales

Sorry all but I am waiting to talk to other retired fishermen, if I can catch one not in a pub, so in the meantime I will tell you a couple of my incidents. One trip in 1975 the cook had to be taken into Shields as his new born daughter had taken bad. It was my first trip as an owner and I did not want to hang about for a man to come up from GY.

Asking around the local dockside pubs I met a Scottish lad, who had missed his boat, Silver Cord, his name Stuart Jensen but we called him Boris, for reasons unknown to me, but I was only the skipper and was treated like a mushroom. Keep me in the dark, and feed me on shit.

Boris had never been on an anchor boat, but he had done a lot of fly shooting, as I said earlier it is the same job fishing with ropes, the only thing he had never seen was the anchor gear, and that is not rocket science.

So off we go, 60 miles off Shields we dropped the anchor and shot the gear, when the net came up there was about six boxes of fish, problem was five of them were small to medium haddock, and only one of flatfish. As we did not keep fish in boxes the haddock were returned to the sea, while I was kicking them through the scupper door, and full of air they floated, Boris was aft helping Taff to set the net for a second haul.

HEY SKIPPER he shouted, "the fish are getting away" Taffy shook his head and told Boris that we did not keep haddock, or small cod for the first ten days, so Boris turned to him and asked how long we were at sea for. When Taffy said that we normally did 15 to 20 days Boris looked stunned, all he said was, " in the name of the wee manny, wait till I tell the boys" he then said to Taffy that if we did not dump everything we caught we would be home a lot faster.

If all fishing boats were like anchor boats, then the north sea would be thriving with fish, but there you go, and at the end of 16 days, Boris asked me if he could stay with us, so what can we make of that. Also with the mesh size of our net being twice the size of a fly dragger we only caught five boxes of haddock, to dump how many swam free?.

Last night I was reading the second of Fred Normandale,s books, Slack water, they are a must read by the way, anyway he mentioned an anchor boat called the Scanboy, the skipper owner, Paddy Collins was a good mate to me in my early days.

If you sailed with him you would never believe that he was the owner of the boat, after dinner, (the Snibbys did not fish in the dark) he would set the alarm clock for about 3am, and tell the cook not to sleep in, but as paddy was crawling into his bunk, the crafty old bugger used to turn it off again, who was he kidding, he had nobody to answer to so why not set it for six, and let the lads relax. Anyway a brilliant man, and never ever raised his voice at sea. R.I.P. Paddy.

Another great character with his own boat Len Gollins, he had a boat called the Danbrit, he was the first English skipper to take an anchor boat away, but he did not move with the times, so when he was told, (after many years as skipper owner) that by law he had to have an echo sounder fitted he was not happy, Len told the D T I that he had fished for years without one, so why spend money on something that he did not need.

Well the law is the law and Len had a second hand one fitted and after testing it the D T I man was happy. Sorry Department Of Trade And Industry. Months later he was asked what he thought of his new sounder he replied, "at £5.00 a roll for paper I have never had it on" tight old sod.

Another skipper and great friend who was not into wasting money was a man called Nat Herd, his father was also Nat and he owned a boat called the Frem, when young Nat left school he sailed with his dad in the Frem, and took over the boat when his father passed away, he was brought up to be frugal, (tight sod), but sadly with family problems he had to sell the Frem and work as skipper in other boats.

Fishing with the Ropes

In no way was it his lack of fishing that lost him the boat, but I will not go into that. During his skippers time he had a few different boats and always did well, from GY and later North Shields, Nat was a strange man as he never spoke about fishing, even when he had a drink.

Imagine how he felt when one day he walked into the office and was told that a man from South Shields was looking for a skipper, and that the boat was rigged for anchor fishing, Nat then asked the name of the boat. Imagine his face when he was told the Frem, he did take it and after two years he bought it off the owner.

What a strange world this is, I would like to think that old Nat had a ghostly hand in this, so after a few years the Frem was back in the family. He did very well with her but sadly she sank, about 1988 but the crew were safe. To this day Nats stepson is skipper owner of a modern prawn trawler, and guess what he has named it?. Frem W. thank you Paul .

After loosing the Frem Nat bought the Mimosa off Ronny Jensen, and even though she had rope reels on her he never went back to the anchor. I never did ask him why but there you go.

One strange thing about Nat taking over the Mimosa was that she had the up to date computer chart, and not many boats had that at the time,

The new navigation gear was run by GPS, just like the one you use in your car today, as it did not use radio waves, like the Decca it was a lot more accurate, (even at night) well Nat saw that this modern computer was on hire, so not being part of the boat, and a big monthly rental to pay, he had them take it out.

Mimosa still had one of the old Decca navigators, so Nat used that, when I did ask him why, as the GPS was a lot better he said that he had always done ok with the Decca, and at his age it was to late to change all of his old paper charts. His age?? He was only 50.

He also told me that he could put his coffee mug on the chart, but not on a computer.

Trevor J Potter

THE FREM. *This is her going down the slip in South Shields the year that Nat bought her back. On the next page is a mock up Decca chart that we used. Note Nats coffee stains.*

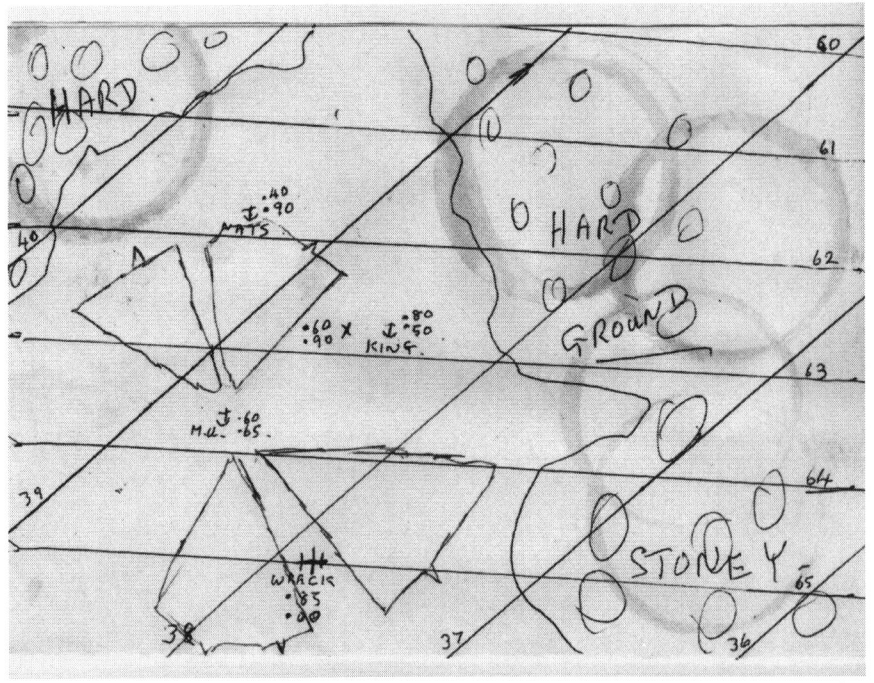

Typical anchor chart.

Fishing with the Ropes

Note the anchor spots have names as well as Decca coordinate numbers, this is so that the lads that worked together when talking on the radio, just said that he was doing ok on the King, or Nats.

There for no actual positions were given out. Crafty old sods but we had to protect our own fishing, all groups of fishing skippers had codes of one sort or another. Also note the coffee stains Well folks I have another chapter ready, but do not worry, I will be back, SORRY but there you go, and I do have to give other fishermen a chance to tell their life on the ropes.

O one last yarn before I go, I have got that Alco simers thingy, so I have forgot it.

Chapter 5 - The Danger

Other than the obvious dangers for all fishing boats, fog, and storms, the gear was the third highest, I bet you are thinking, why have I put Fog first?. Well to me the anchor boat was built with storms in mind, but fog is the fishermen's first worry, I have heard a lot of skippers say that they would rather have a gale of wind any day.

Especially for a wooden boat, as they made very bad radar reflectors a steel trawler will show up on all radar screens, where as an anchor boat, in choppy weather made a very bad target. All the wooden boats would have a metal radar reflector on the top of the mast, but to be honest that did not help much, then there was the fact that with being at anchor you had less chance of getting out of another targets way.

Also if you had the fishing gear out, well the chance of moving was almost zero, imagine an anchor at the front of you and a set of fishing gear behind you then where can you go?. Before radar got to be as good as it is today, like in the 60s and early 70s, the likely hood of a boat picking us up on their radar was, well put it this way winning the lottery is more likely.

When Bob McQueen was skipper of a boat called Ella Grethe while laid at anchor in fog, the lads were on the deck sorting the fish, Bob was in the wheelhouse, he told me he was sorting his chart out ready for shooting the next haul, but I have sailed with bob and found him to be allergic to work. All of a sudden Bang, they had been hit by a large merchant ship, the big boats bow was stuck in-between the two halves of the Ella, luckily the big boat did not go astern, if she had then Bobs boat would have sunk instantly.

His crew told me later that Bob jumped on top of his wheelhouse then up on the ships stem, it was a case of fu** you jack I am ok, the lads were then taken on to the ship and safety, the snibby sank in a matter of minutes. If the crew had not been on deck they would not have been there to tell me the story, lucky lads.

As I said earlier the crew of the Pecewave were not so lucky when they got hit in fog, as they were in their bunks. Another snibby that was sunk in thick fog was the Arcona Champion. This boat had finished her trip and was at anchor in the Humber river, only about half a mile off Grimsby waiting for the lock gates to open.

She had a good trip of fish and the crew were washed and dressed ready to go ashore. Then out of the fog came a deep sea trawler from Hull again the crew were lucky as when the trawler hit her the crew were on deck, and were picked up. That is a bit of a sickener as they had worked a full trip and lost the lot.

Ar Acona Champion

It makes you wonder how many other boats that were lost without trace over the years had been victims of a collision and NOT the storms.

Another big danger on the anchor, was before we got the rope reels as the ropes were stacked on the deck, and being shot away the mate had to stand aft to make sure that no knots went over, as this would spoil the fishing when heaving the gear in. this is because if we had to stop the ropes then the fish would swim free while the gear was static. Wow that's a posh word for me.

If a tangled rope did go over the side then the mate would take a turn on the post and that would normally pull it clear, if not the skipper went astern and the knot was pulled back on board, and then cleared

Sadly over the years a few men went over the side while trying to clear the rope and were not saved. To me the rope reels not only made the job easy, they made it a hell of a lot safer.

One young lad that had a bad mishap was called Alan White, when he was cook on the Danbrit, on the deck alone looking after the first three coil being heaved in, (this was the normal practice) a knot or twist came up in the rope, instead of stopping the winch he tried to clear it himself. Now we have all done the same but it is a bad idea, the twist did unravel but he had his hand in the midst of it. He was pulled over the rail, and then into the side roller, well he lost his arm from the elbow, he was a lucky lad. That may sound a daft thing to say, but he could have been killed dead.

Anyway he went on to work for the firm of Danbrit fish sales, as the ships runner, maybe that was a blessing in disguise as he had a decent job for a lot of years to come. When I first joined the anchor boats in 1965 on the Maxwell, a knot in the ropes was called an Englishman, when I ask why I was told that the early Danish skippers said that only the English lads stacked the ropes in a fashion that they would go foul. To me that is taking the piss, but even with a full English crew we still shouted ENGLISHMAN, when a rope came up foul.

Another massive danger was the whipping barrels on the winch, if you were unlucky enough to get your oil skins caught between the rope and the drum, well it was good bye, and that happened to a lot of men. That is the reason that on a snibby we wore a short top and waterproof trousers, as the trawler style long oilskin frocks were too much of a danger. It was not until the mid 1980s that it became a law to have a guard over the barrels, to be honest all the family owned boats had them fitted before then.

I know this CHAPTER is not funny, but one day on the Maxwell, while watching the first three coil I decided to peel the spuds, the bucket had a length of rope on so that I could draw water from over the rail, as I was stepping over the incoming ropes, bucket in hand all of a sudden it was pulled away from me. Yep I had left the rope dangling and It went round the whipping barrel. I had to stop the winch and when the skipper came on deck, well put it this way, my ears were burning for a whole week. It was also mashed spuds for dinner.

Another danger in this type of boat was when we were dropping the anchor. In fine weather most skippers dropped the anchor while going full astern, in bad weather this was not possible, as the boat would automatically put her stern into the wind, so we then had to go ahead.

Doing this there was always the danger of the anchor wire jumping out of the forward roller, in the boats stem, the man stood forward to attach the anchor floats had to make sure that he was in a safe position, in the event of this happening. To be honest I was amazed at the amount of men that did not, I was sick of shouting "STAND ASTERN OF THE RIGGING", but for some reason they never saw the danger.

One day on a boat called the Halton we were dropping anchor, with a big swell running and the wire did jump out, Taffy was stood in the wrong place and the wire had him pinned to the forward post.

I screamed to the mate (Billy Macutchin) to keep the wire running as slack as he could, meanwhile the cook Paddy Walsh was pulling the wire away from Taffys body. If the mate had panicked and stopped the winch, Taff would have instantly had been cut in two.

With luck and fast thinking from the two lads Taffy had time to drop to the deck, and safety.

Paddys hands were cut to ribbons, but he did save Taffys life.

SKANDERBORG.

I LOST THIS BOAT IN A STORM IN 1983. the full story of that is in my first book GRANDAD BOATS. But back to the fog, note the radar reflector, this boat had a metal wheelhouse so that helped but a boat with a wooden wheelhouse, that tiny thing at the top of the mast was the only target. It was about one foot square.

And a lot of boats that had it blown off the mast never replaced it, so then there was no radar target at all, it amazes me that today I can go on my computer and not only see the boats at sea, but there names beside it. How mad is that, to be honest I am glad that this was not the case in my days as I always said that I was fishing in another area and nobody could call me a liar. Not that I ever did, lie that is, my fingers are crossed lads.

Most days the first haul in the morning was shot by just two men, giving the others an extra hour or two in their bunks, this was normal on most boats but you had to take your time when shooting the net, as if one man went over with the net then the other one had a VERY slim chance of getting him back.

One very silly, NO, stupid skipper used to shoot the gear all by himself, one day the crew awoke to find the boat (BENNISON) had no Skipper, she was going ahead at slow speed, so it was presumed that he went over with the net. Sometimes you can be too kind.

I have just been told by Egon Thomsen that the skippers name was Robert Thinnesen, R.I.P.

photo from Grimsby telegraph.

I have added this picture as it shows how the ropes were stowed in the early days, before the rope reels, it shows how easy it was for a rope to go foul, and take a man overboard.

Chapter 6 - The Skippers Good And Bad

All men are different, but to me skippers come in three category's, first the silent one as you never know where you stand with them, next the bigheads, they are always shouting and screaming and this makes for a long and unhappy trip, last but the best are the men who go out to earn money, but also respect the fact that they need a crew to do that. So the respect is returned by the lads.

I have seen men leave a top earning boat, and sign up with a mid earner, (known as a plodder) that was because they made a living and the crew had a happy life.

Do not get me wrong, a lot of the top men were gents, but sadly there was a few that looked at the crew like sh★★.

My first skipper was Jack Clark (Canadian Jack) as he was from Wick in Scotland, I never did ask why Canadian, very easy going but if something went wrong he would loose his temper BIG time. But never with the crew, we had to smile and look away while he was kicking the wheelhouse door, or any thing else that happened to be at hand, or should I say FOOT.

But what made him so strange, was after his tantrum he would be extra nice to us on the deck, maybe he felt guilty for his outburst. But it was never aimed at the crew. I do remember one Sunday the mate and I wanted a sub, (money for a pint), with the office being closed we went round to Jacks house to ask him. When we got there we saw a Childs tent on the front lawn and sticking out of the flap was a pair of feet

Any way the night before Jacks wife had locked him out, we woke him up and asked for some money, when he looked his wallet was missing. Then Masie his wife came to the door and asked what we wanted she knew really but was making Jack sweat it out.

When he told her that he had lost his wallet, she smiled and said that she had it. She then gave Barry and me £5.00 each, on the understanding that hubby did not get a penny off us, well with us fishermen sticking together we took the money and said our goodbye's to our skipper. As we were walking out of his garden all I herd was "you two bastards are sacked".

His boat the Maxwell was a good age, but when the office offered him a brand new boat, he turned them down, very strange but he did tell me that he felt safe in her, so why change, VERY TRUE.

The next skipper for me was a lad named Jerry Lee, he had a boat called Katherine Jean, now jerry was one of the silent types, I did two trips with him and I do not think he said more than a dozen words, all he ever said was set the alarm for 3AM, and every haul, LET GO. (of the anchor gear that is) otherwise you would think he was a mute, all he did all day and even eating his dinner, was read cowboy books, another thing I never ever saw that man in a public house. But he was well liked by all who sailed with him.

My third skipper was Barry Emerson, his boat was the Ling bank, wow talk about chalk and cheese, Barry never ever stopped talking, and I think it was a nerve thing, every thing aboard Ling Bank was top speed. And sometimes too fast for the crew. I remember well that as we were heaving the bag of fish on board, we had to let go and he started to shoot the next haul. We still had the fish in the cod end and Barry was shooting the ropes.

The next skipper I sailed with was Mick Jensen, on a boat called East Bank, now this lad really loved himself, a very strange man, he was known throughout the fleet as Captain Cannonball, was to find out later why that was.

Now most skippers, if they made a mistake they would admit it, but not Mick, do not get me wrong we did have the odd laugh but I do think that most of the time it was aimed at him. What a strange guy, one day sat down the cabin the subject of class came up.

He said to the crew that they were lower class and that he was middle class, at first they thought he was joking, but no he was deadly serious, so the cook Barry Isherwood asked him why?.

Mick replied that as he owned half of the boat and they were working for him, that made the class difference, also he had a mortgage, and the crew lived in council houses. Where the fuck was this guys head, and he never realised that even the other skippers and owners had no time for him.

Going back to the dangers, dropping the anchor. One fine day Mick was getting ready to drop anchor, I was at the winch, and the cook stood forward as normal, ready to chain the anchor bladders on.

Steaming full ahead the skipper shouted let go, and this I did, while the wire was running out I was thinking to myself that the boat should by now be slowed down, but no we were still going full speed just as the first shackle came off the drum, the one that I had to stop so the bladder could be attached, the engine then eased to slow, but the 50 TON boat was still flying through the water.

Now if I had stopped the winch one of three things would have happened, 1 we would part the wire, 2 we would have ripped the forward rail off, or 3 the winch would have been damaged BIG time.

Anyway I shouted to the cook to jump clear and decided not to stop the winch, but let the cable run. I then saw that Mick had turned the boat hard to starboard and stopped the winch.

The skipper shouted to me "why the fuck did you not stop the winch" I had to smile at this and replied, "sorry Mick I was daydreaming, as we all do at times" he knew that I was taking the piss but he decided to let it drop. As the old saying goes the skipper is NEVER wrong, that was forty years ago, so if you are reading this Mick I hope you have calmed down.

The next man I sailed with Poul Sorensen, the first Danish skipper I had been with, it was in a boat called the Dorny, and she only had a one cylinder Tuxham engine, very strange sound, especially if I was stood aft. I got a big surprise at this man, he was always laughing and joking, and in the one year that I was with him, we never shot more than four hauls a day.

His preferred fishing area was the Dogger Bank, so it was all top quality flat fish, and he made a lot of money, and like I said a gentleman to sail with.

A few years later when I had a boat of my own, we landed the same day as the Dorny, and she was full to the hatch, plus another 30 to 40 kits on her deck, I said to him "hey Poul where did you get that lot from?" he smiled at me and answered, "Trevor you sailed with me for a full season so if you did not copy the fishing charts while you were on watch then you are the daft one". Everybody called him little Poul, to me he was a big man.

The next and last man I sailed with, before I started skipper was Mac the teacher, every one called him this for the simple reason that was his profession, before he decided to go fishing. I sailed with this man for two years, when I ask him why he gave up a good job to go fishing, he told me that he was sick of kids holding their hands up and asking if they could use the toilet.

His actual words were "if they want a piss why ask" he also said that he sometimes felt like saying no, now I know that is not the real reason that he gave up a steady job but I did not bother going any further as I knew he would tell me another heap of crap.

The fleet may have called him the teacher in jest, but to me he was the best teacher in the world. When he realised that I was looking to go skipper in the future, well he put himself out and gave me loads of help. The first thing he taught me was to always respect the crew, and then they would return the respect, another strange thing about Mac was that he always knew when the lads were a bit down and it did not take him long to pick up their spirits, like in bad weather as we were dragging the ropes away, he would start a sing song, he would shout out of the wheelhouse, (not singing, but speaking the words) on top of old smoky , then us lads would sing that line, all covered in snow, then we would again sing that line. By the time the song was over we forgot how wet and cold we were.

TEACHER? He should have been a psychologist, but it worked every time. He was also just like little Poul (Dorny), slow and relaxed fishing. One thing he used to say when the fishing was slack, "take the anchor up lads, I feel like a change of scenery" well all I could see was the sea and the sky, how the fuck can you change that without going inshore.

Mac was a man who liked to fish well north, so the only time we saw another anchor boat was steaming home. He worked that far north that in a 20 day trip 4 of them we were steaming, but in two years I never landed without a decent wage.

Popping back to Mick (cannonball) one day I asked him if I could try picking up the dhan, and clipping up to the anchor gear, this sounds pretty straight forward, but with the weight of the fishing gear behind the boat it was not so easy. Plus you had to take care not to get the rope in the propeller while going astern. Coming up to the dhan with Mick stood behind me I was a bit nervy, it did not help with him telling me faster, slower, more wheel, and then he took the wheel off me and told me that I needed more practice. Now if I did, I was not going to get it off him.

Back on Coral Bank, it was my second trip, Mac asked me if I had ever shot the gear away before, I told him no, so he said that it was time to start, as in the case of him dropping dead then I could finish the trip.

So after a few little bits of advise he then went onto the deck, it was good weather and all went to plan, Mac then said "thank you now I can have a nap in the afternoon while you take a haul.

As he always worked a man below he could now have a haul off himself. All went well for a week, then we had a bad weather day, so I did not expect Mac to turn in for the afternoon haul, but he did.

I shot the gear all was ok until I came to pick up the dahn, then every thing went wrong, with the wind and swell I missed the dhan, then I got the rope in the propeller.

With luck it did not cut it, so we managed to throw the hand grapple and pick up the other end, I then took turns on the aft post and put the prop in gear. That cut the rope free, we then had another go at the dhan, and this time I managed it. It normally takes about ten minutes to clip up to the anchor and start heaving, well this episode took me about an hour. I could not understand why Mac did not wake up with all the commotion, when I opened his cabin door, (his bunk was behind the wheelhouse), there he was sat on the chart table smoking a fag.

When I started to tell him about the fuck up that I had made he smiled and said "we all make them now and them" he had been sat watching every thing through his porthole. He then told me that I had handled the whole thing well.

I could not make up my mind whether to thank him or hit him, how many skipper owners would sit and watch a beginner loose a set of ropes and also the haul. Now that was the biggest confidence boost any man could wish for. Thanks for that Mac.

Dennis McKenny, along with a skipper from North Shields, Robin Crawford, (M.F.V Border Maid) got together and was a leading factor in organising the blockade in 1975. sadly that did no good at all as we were now under the E.U. and our government had no interest in backing us. As we saw in the two major cod wars off Iceland. But at least those men who ran the blockade of all UK ports gave it a try. And with a lot of skippers turning against them, well they just did not bother to carry on the fight.

To me if we had any backing from our government, all those men would have been heroes, but instead they were forgotten. I will tell you one thing, knowing Mac as I did I saw a big change in him, he was not the same man, he had lost his spark, and his will to fight.

A couple of years after that he sold his boat and bought a fish restaurant.

This next pic is of the snibbys blockading Immingham docks, the ferry waiting to get in is the Tor Hollandia, while she was tying up she hit one of the fishing boats Scanboy, and bent her aft mast, I think most of the damage was to the ferry captains pride. And the fact that he had to lay there for a few days before the stupid English fishermen would let him enter.

I did make a mental note not to travel on that ferry for my holidays.

picture Grimsby Telegraph.

When I started skipper, with Mac giving so much advice and help, a lot of the other skippers called me little Mac, at first this annoyed me but thinking on, it was something to be proud of as I was using his charts and his mode of fishing, well I could see where they were coming from, and were I was going too.

Another skipper I must tell you about, even though I never sailed with him, Johnny Abbot, he was a strange chap, and I never did hear him on the VHF even when he was fishing close to us. And at times that could be very annoying as on the North East Bank we had to let the other guys know where our gear was, over the years a few skippers got tangled up with his gear.

Now he did not have to chat, but at least talk to the other lads about his gear. Maybe he did not give a shit about his own set of ropes as the government paid for them. But he could have had a thought for other boats, but there you go.

If you are wondering why the government paid for his ropes, the lucky old man had a contract, if ever there was an airplane or boat had any type of mishap, then he would use his ropes to help them, so all his ropes were paid for.

Fishing with the Ropes

Had to show this as it is a sad ending for a great boat, IRIS DEAN.

Chapter 7 - James Purdy Cullen

This next story was given to me by a good friend and shipmate, he has asked me not to change it in any way, and after reading it I do not think that I should, Jimmy was on a few anchor boats in the 60s, and one that springs to my mind was a trip he did on the Katherine Jean. A boat that I had been on flat fishing, skipper Jerry Lee, they sailed on 21/08/1968, and landed 7 days later, so that meant fishing time of only three days they landed 365, 10 stone kits. All big cod

In 1966 Jim moved to a boat called the Brig that sounds a familiar name, old Karl must have had us all with him at on time or another,

Ok all I will now pass you over to Jimmy as I said he wants to tell you this bit himself, well I never could shut him up, so I am off

For a pint and leave him to it.

REEF BANK GY 619.

November 1969 we sailed from Grimsby early morning, it was to be a trip that I will never forget, I had been in the Reef Bank for a while the skipper, Peter Oust, Benny McCuthchon mate, I was deckhand, and the cook was a lad called Dick Morrel..

It was to be the last trip of the year and we started fishing on the tail end of the Dogger Bank there were a few boats, Peter had been speaking on the radio with his brother, Berger Oust, he was fishing well and staying on the same anchor spot, advised his brother to come and take over from him.

Fishing with the Ropes

We arrived, dropped our anchor and got ready to shoot the first haul, we were working 14 coil of rope each side of the net, the first ropes went ok, then the net went all clear, but while shooting the second fleet of rope a large tangle, (Englishman) started to go aft and jammed against the rail.

All rope men have it brayed into them that you never try to keep a foul rope inboard , first thing is to let it go over then catch a turn on the aft towing post, most times the rope would then pull itself clear.

While shooting the ropes off the forward deck, as they had to run past the winch, also the side rollers we used a length of chain from the bottom of the winch to the boats rail, this chain stopped the rope from catching on the rollers and the winch. And one Golden rule while shooting, you NEVER, NEVER, step over the guard chain while the ropes are running, the thing you must do is run down the starboard side and then catch a turn, I knew while I was doing it that I should not be, anyway as I stepped over the chain I put my foot into a foul rope.

Of all the stupid things I have done in my life, well this one takes the top prize, all those years having been shouted at and having it drummed into me I broke the Cardinal rule. Do not step over the chain.

As my boot hit the deck I knew that I was in the shit, I had stood into a bight of the foul rope, it gripped my left foot like a vice, I was going over the guard chain backwards the rope tightened with the drag of the gear I was being pulled aft, I was gone, I bashed my face on the shooting bar. I was aware of screams but did not know where from, I remember my legs going around the bar, after that nothing.

The next bit of this should be told by one of the others, (but sadly they are no longer with us).

As I went overboard the skipper put the wheel hard over to port, then Benny managed to catch a turn with the rope on the aft end post, with the boat going hard over it eased the strain on the rope, Benny kept slacking it a bit at a time, if he had not, then I would have been cut in two, or lost my leg.

By this time I was aware of water in my face and great pain, the next thing I remember was being grabbed by the hair (yes I did have some then) what had happened was incredible, the foul rope had pulled clear, and spat me out, the air in my oilskin top brought me to the surface, kept me afloat while Peter the skipper had managed to get me along side he then grabbed me by the hair and pulled me back onboard.

While all this was going on I was dead to any pain, what was going on around me, well I do not know but it all happened in the space of 20 minuets or so. When I did eventually come round the pain o the pain, I thought that every bone in my body was broken.

The lads cut off my oilskins and one boot, (the other one was missing,) and the pain in my leg was horrendous, every time they tried to move me was agony, so they decided to leave me on the deck wrapped in a flock mattress and blankets. I think it must have been the fastest the gear had ever been hauled in one ended, just as well it was a fine morning.

Every 4 to 5 mins one of the lads came and spoke to me, or to check on me, the pain was horrendous , not only from my lower body but my face as well, I could feel my face swelling up and my right eye was completely closed. I must have passed out again as when I woke up I was in the bunk behind the wheelhouse, I was in agony, Benny was sat on the deck beside me, I did not know what I was doing.

I was crying for my Mam, imagine that a grown man crying for his Mam, did not feel the needle going in, but boy did it do it's job Peter was talking to his brother Berger Oust, I did not have a care in the world, (morphine is a great pain killer).

I don't know how long we were steaming but the lifeboat came along side, they had a doctor on board and after checking me over he told them to call for the helicopter. I was transferred to the lifeboat and strapped into a basket ready for the lift, the pain was starting again but they gave me another shot of morphine.

I was then lifted up to the chopper, I was more terrified of going up on the wire with the fly guy than I care to remember, all I can say is fantastic aircrew, I cannot thank those guys enough, a short time later we landed at Scartho road hospital.

The most embarrassing thing of the whole thing was when they cut the rest of my clothes off I had sh** myself, what seemed like an age of being rolled over one way then the other fingers poking and hands squeezing they sent me for x rays. I was on gas and air, it was great stuff, well both my legs were broken and one arm, plus I had the best black eyes that I had ever seen, or tried to see.

Fishing with the Ropes

After the operation I came round in intensive care and a young nurse said that I looked more like a mummy than a fisherman. After a couple of days they moved me onto a ward, Benny and Dick came to see me with sweeties and fruit, we sat and talked about the incident, not that I could remember much about it. All I do know is that these guys had saved my life. Benny told me that the skipper would be up the next day.

The mission man had drove down from Shields, bringing my mother with him, when she saw me she broke her heart, ma stayed with me all day and that evening the mission man took her back home, thank you.

The next day Peter Oust came in and gave me the biggest rollicking ever, and also told me that I was sacked. Well I would not be going to sea for a long time, so getting the sack was no bother. I had lots of visitors over the next five weeks, and the mission came in every second day with new clothes and whatever I needed.

One visitor was a bit embarrassing , his name Billy Grant, he lived in North Shields, but was on one of the deep sea trawlers fishing from Hull. Bill was a strange guy, nobody was safe from his sense of humour, and his way of getting the nurse's attention was "Hey custard crutch I am looking for a lad named Jimmy Cullen" how embarrassing, but they took him in good fun, he was the sort of man that could get away with his cheek, as it was not personal.

He had brought me 12 cans of bonded Guinness and two tins of Old Friend tobacco, after I told him the story and how it happened all he said was "serve's you right thanks for the sympathy Billy.

After a while I was getting stronger, flying around in a wheel chair they decided to send me to a hospital in Shields, and I was amazed at the amount of visitors that came to see me friends and family.

Then I was eventually discharged in September 1970. that was 43 years ago, and even today if I am walking along the fish quay I will not step over a length of chain.

One last and very sad thing five year later Billy McCutchon went over the side of another anchor boat, Morena, and was never seen again. R.I.P. Billy my friend. Jim Cullen.

Hi all I am back, tell you what Jimmy was a very lucky lad, when you think of how many men were lost with the gear, especially in the early days, before the rope reels.

Time to head back to Shields and talk to a couple of Fly Dragging skippers as I do not want to be told that the anchor men hogged all the book.

REEF BANK AFTER THE NEW ROPE REELS.

Chapter 8 - Terry Fairley

Terry Fairley. Was the first fly shooting skipper that I talked to, like I said earlier Shields had both anchor boats and fly shooters, now in GY there was no fly shooters at all. He was born in 1940 in North Shields, (so that makes him a Geordie) and went to Linskill high school, so that gives the school at least one success story.

At the age of 10 he used to go to sea pleasure tripping on the old drifters, Young John and Wydale, and then on the seine net boats Our Lassie, Gracie and a few others. One of them was the Poseidon, I bet he was glad that it was not the big one that turned over.

I can tell already that this lad was destined to spend his life at sea. In his spare time Terry would help the local store W. White's by delivering stores to the different boats, as well as the few shillings that he got off them, he would also get a few fish off each boat, and made more money selling it from door to door.

In the school holidays at the age of 11 he went to sea on a boat called the Gracie,

One day he was going down the ladder to the boat, at low tide, in Shields that is a 25 foot drop, the skipper Norman Morse was coming down behind him when he fell, onto the boats rail, then onto one of the beams, Terry pulled him aboard and the harbour master came to give him a helping hand he had broken both of his legs, when the ambulance arrived, Norman said to Terry, "when you leave school there is a job waiting for you".

Sadly in the east coast harbours, a lot of men were lost trying to get on the boat at low water. North Shields is the most notorious as many a man was lost, after braving the bad weather at sea and to get lost in the harbour to me was as bad as it gets.

On leaving school in 1955 Terry did go on the Duen with Norman Morse and was paid £3.00 a week, they were anchor bashing from the port of Sunderland, most of the fishing in them days was done close to the land, as there was no need to steam miles out to find fish. But one trip they did go further out 60 mile.

With no electric gear in those days they towed a log line behind them this was a small propeller that turned and then recorded the boats speed, and distance travelled. They then dropped a lead line, with a dab of grease on the bottom, this told them how deep the water was, and also the type of bottom they were in, if the grease was clean then they knew the bottom was hard, but they were looking for sand stuck to it, hey all clever stuff.

One day they got up at daylight and could not start the engine, there were no other boats in the area, for a tow so they put the sail up, it took them three days to sail back to the Tyne, five miles to go and the skippers son Alan came out and towed them the last five mile.

Terry told me that if the water looked cloudy, they would tie a pint size mug to a length of twine, as they lowered it into the sea if you lost sight of it after two fathom then it was too murky for the ropes to do the job so they then moved to deeper water.

I have been told this same story off a lot of the older fishermen so I know that it was widely used, it was called a potometer, I wonder why?. One day on the Duan the fishing was very slack so we decided to go back into Sunderland. As we neared the harbour there was a small swell running and no wind, but on the bar we could see the sea breaking.

It was a big breaker so the skipper told the mate to put 6 baskets on a coil of rope, and tow it astern now the idea of this is if the engine stopped or if a large breaker hit you this would act as a sea anchor and stop the boat going broadside, but we did hit a big breaker and the rope that we were towing parted. Well we were off like a bullet.

(still no wind) but we had to don our life jackets and stay on the deck In all my years at sea since this happened I have never seen it again,

Fishing with the Ropes

I have been told that it was a freak tidal rip, that is when the tide fights the swell. Thank god there was no wind.

1956 the anchor boat Elk. Still with Terry.

The first trip on the Elk, the very first haul he went into the cabin, aft and found about three foot of water, there was smoke coming from the gearbox on the engine, so he had to stop her, to attract attention to other boats they heaved a blanket, soaked in fuel and set it alight, sadly this set the spare net that was on top of the wheelhouse alight, as there was not many boats in the area, there was not a lot of hope.

Well we were sinking and now the wheelhouse was well afire, so not being daft they got the lifeboat outboard.

Luckily a boat called the Snowflake saw the smoke, came along side and put the fire out with the deck hose, and then towed the Elk back to the river Tyne.

Can I stop for a second, Look I have only typed two pages of Terry's life, and by fuck I am glad that I never sailed with him. Also the book so far seems to be full of trouble and accidents. WELL THAT WAS TRUE FISHING.

In 1957 Terry went down to GY to start on the anchor boats from there, after a couple of trips on the Botney Cut, he then joined a boat called Danbrit. That name is familiar ? most of us have sailed on her at one time or other. She had just sailed from Denmark, after having a new engine fitted.

When they sailed the skipper Eric Swainson, decided to try a days fishing off the coast of Denmark, just to be sure that all the new gear was running ok, as it was the fishing was great, so they fished the whole trip there.

Steaming home they were crossing the notorious Dogger Bank, when they were hit by a south easterly storm, the weather was that bad (and steaming broad side to the wind) the skipper decided to drop anchor, and put the storm chain out.

VERY sensible move, with the bank being very shoal (it does not let the anchor spring chain work too well) the skipper had to use the propeller to help take the strain off the anchor gear. as if things could not get any worse, the sail broke lose and was flapping about like a whip. In bad storms all skippers take the sail down as it is safer without one but if you are hit by a freak storm, sometimes rather than risk loosing a man, well they take a chance and leave it up.

Any way now they had to get it down, but the skipper decided it was safer to tell the crew to cut it away, as it was cracking like a whip, and causing the boat to shake badly. Terry told me that when the storm chain pulled tight he thought that was his lot.

After the storm died down they finished their journey to GY, while the fish were being landed someone asked how we got seaweed on the aerials at the top of the mast, it was the remains of the sail.

There were a few boats with damage from that freak storm, and sadly one was lost. Terry then decided to go back home to North Shields, the boats from his home town tended to do shorter trips than the anchor bashers in GY.

Terry spent the next few years sailing with the Morse family, they owned a few boats, all starting with con, now that would put me off straight away, Contester, Condowen, Conmoran, and later years a few more, he had the same sort of accident as Jim Cullen, getting caught in a foul rope, but he came off lightly. Getting a foul rope wrapped around his hand while shooting away on the Contester he was lucky that it pulled clear before dragging him overboard, I say lucky, he lost one finger, and broke another two.

He also told me that in those years he went overboard twice, and got pulled back. Another time they had a rope in the propeller, so he dived over and cut it free, his back was cut to ribbons with the barnacles on the hull, but it saved them getting towed back in, I just hope they bought him a drink for saving the trip.

Any way while he was recovering from loosing his finger he decided to sit for his skippers ticket. Hey I do not blame you mate, get in the wheelhouse, and keep out of mischief.

After getting his ticket Terry's first boat was called the Lively Hope, on his first trip he decided to try the gear close inland. So just one hour off the Tyne he caught 120 boxes of fish, lucky sod.

He did three years in her and did very well. Then he took a brand new boat the Cherry Burton. Newington trawlers had about six new boats, all called ????? Burton or Burton ???????????? I cannot list them all. But Terry was to take another new boat the BISHOP BURTON.

Fishing with the Ropes

And he had her for a long time, often getting his name in the fishing news, for top landings of fish.

At first she had no rope reels, so the ropes came through the Beccles coiler and into the forward part of the fish room, called the bins. This idea was not as successful as stacking the rope by hand, sometimes if the rope went foul it would take two or three hours to clear them.

Then after a while they had the reels fitted, imagine the time saved, and the safety aspect, money well spent. The Bishop was built to take on any type of fishing, Fly shooting / trawling / and even for a time mackerel fishing out of Penzance.

On march 27 1980, while fishing in an area about 200 miles north east of the Tyne, fishing was very good but the weather was bad, a strong north-westerly wind, Terry also noticed that the tide was running against the wind all day, not often seen but when it does happen it confuses the waves, and that is when you get a lot more rouge waves.

Then he heard a MAY-DAY being given out, now in that area there is a large oil and gas complex, called Ekofisk. At that time there was about ten rigs in a small area, today 2012 it is massive, like a town in the middle of the sea.

One of the rigs Alexander Kielland had capsized into the sea, one of the legs had given way, there were a lot of fishing boats in the area and all went to assist. The Bishop was asked to search in an area north west of the toppled rig, they never saw anyone all night but sadly, in the daylight they picked up four bodies.

Alan Morse, Congener found the leg off the rig it was floating upside down, and Cliff Ellis, Christine Neilson picked up one of the life saving baskets from the rig, there was a young lad in it but he had died with the cold conditions.

H M S Lindisfarne took all the bodies off the fishing boats so they then carried on with the job of fishing. There was a loss of 123 men that night, and the normal banter between the boats fishing was non existing.

Well that is all Terry has written down for me, but like most top earning fishermen, he has not mentioned the times that he broke the port record. Also like I said I never sailed with him, but speaking to a lot

Trevor J Potter

of his ex crewmen, they have a Very high regard for him. Most of them told me he was a nutter, in fishing that is high praise.

A North Shields trawler has landed a record catch of 730 boxes of cod and made £16000.00 for a six day trip,

Terry

Fishing with the Ropes

Chapter 9 - Ray Morse

Ray was born in 1945 he was an adopted son to the Morse family and they were a big influence on starting the fly shooting in North Shields. Well to be exact they started with anchor boats.

Norman John Morse had a boat called Garcia in 1948. his son Norrie also started with an anchor boat called the Noel C, that one sunk after damage to the stern gland, they had a full coil of rope in the propeller.

As time went on the family invested in two boats, to fish from North Shields, Starting out as anchor boats, later converted to fly shooting.

They called them Concord and Contester.

With the ground off the north east coast having a lot of hard spots they decided that fly shooting was a better way of fishing. In the early days you did not need to go far off shore to catch fish, in in 1959 after a lot of success they had another boat built, and this one was named Conmoran

All the sons and brothers had one of the boats, at one time or another but for some reason Ray did not fit into their plans. So in 1966 he decided to make his own way in fishing, and move down to GY.

Rays first job was in the Katherine Jean, with Jerry Lee, another one of my old skippers. In 1967 he decided to sit for his skippers ticket, and he did that in South Shields. After getting it he went back to GY and sailed with a man named Oger Lund. The boat was called Tanana, a very successful skipper and I take it that you have guessed that he was

Danish, (the name is a clue) sorry, anyway Ray was to spend four years with him and also took the boat away on a couple of relief trips.

After doing ok with the Tanana the office gave him a start of his own, she was called Eastards, he was to go on to do four years as skipper of her, and they were obviously happy with his earnings, the only time I kept a boat for that long was when I had paid for it.

I then went on to ask Ray if he had any funny or bad tales to tell me, one was about the whale playing with the ropes,(same as Ron Jenson) but this time Fred as we called the whale, came up in-between the ropes and blew the air out, what a smell that was. Another funny incident was while fishing on the North East Bank, with Ray living in North Shields, on a Saturday evening he would steam the five hours and spend Sunday at home lucky sod.

Sail on the night time and be back to his anchor for daylight on Monday. He never invited me so on Sunday I would use his anchor and give the ground around mine a rest, he told me later that he knew I was doing this but it did not spoil his dinner.

I then asked him of any scary times that he had, (as we all did) he told me that one storm he got caught in was very nasty, he was fishing the east side of the north sea when he got hit by a storm force wind, while at anchor, riding out the storm she took a bad one.

At the time he was stood in the wheelhouse, all he could see was the mast, everything else was under water, he then put her in gear and went full ahead. To me this saved his boat, slowly she came up, but the boat was full of water, and no wheelhouse windows left intact, also all his electronic gear was fu**ed.

They were very lucky lads, if Ray had not gone full ahead, WELL.

Can I stop for a moment?. Have you noticed that every man I have talked to in this book, have told me about STORMS, and Bad damage, to you it may sound mad, but to those fishermen it was part of the job, not a nice part but there you go.

Also there were a lot of men that were not so lucky, the ones that never got to tell the tale.

Fishing with the Ropes

The Eastards, imagine everything under water, except for the top half of the wheelhouse, and the mast. They also lost the life raft in the same wave.

Being closer to Denmark than England Ray decided to go in to Esbejerg for repairs. On his way in with no navigational gear working, he got on the wrong side of a very bad sand bank, it is called Horn Reef, and it has claimed a few boats in the past. He was very lucky that day as the North Sea ferry Dana Regina was sailing and the captain told Ray the course he had to steam to get back into the deep water channel.

The pilot boat then escorted them into safe harbour. It took two weeks to do all the repair work, on completion the Eastards was iced and stored up ready for another trip, or so they thought, when they sailed and clearing the channel, as he got alongside the light ship, there was a medium swell running she dipped her nose and then on riding up the next wave (you will find this hard to believe) any way riding up the next wave the main mast fell down, smashing the wheelhouse and all the aerials came down with it. well you have got to laugh.

That could only happen in the Pirates of the Caribbean. Anyway about turn and back in to Denmark for more lager. The mast had been broken in the big storm, with the rigging holding it upright they never noticed it. Tit heads, (I am talking about the shipyard workers).

Ray had the Eastards for four years, you do not keep a boat out of GY, that length of time unless the owner is happy.

Raymond Morse. Ray I have adjusted the pic so you look thinner, you can get me a pint later.

He also told me that the ten years spent in GY, were the happiest time of his whole career. 1980 Ray moved back to his home town of N Shields, but still never took one of the family boats.

Ray took a prawn trawler called the Achieve for a year or two, then his brother Norrie decided to retire from the fishing.

The Conduan had the rope reels taken off and spent the rest of her days trawling. Ray took over skipper of her and stayed with her until he retired.

His other nephew Alan, who was the skipper owner of a very large steel fly shooter/ trawler, sadly dropped dead while at sea. He was in his early 40s.

Both Ray and I agree that it was the worry of the big loan and the dwindling fishing industry that caused his heart failure.

Fishing with the Ropes

CONGENER. R.I.P Alan Morse.

Chapter 10 - The Crew

Now we come to the most important part of a fishing boat, and that is the lad that worked the deck, they came in all types of men, the miseries, those that never made it as skipper, the contented, they were the ones that did not want the worry of being a skipper, and last but to me the best. The nutters and piss artists.

And they are the ones that worked their hearts out just to make some money. A lot of skippers used to say "I do not want him, he drinks too much" well I say give him to me then, as he works like a horse.

I have said it before and I say it again, show them respect, and it is returned. I remember one trip in the Bennison, fishing from Shields we had a decent trip onboard but the last day fishing was very bad, average of 1 box per haul, it was a flat calm sunny day and we were going to land the next morning.

I put my head out of the window and said to the lads, "ok guys we can have two more hauls and get in for midnight, or go home now and have a couple of pints before landing" it went to a vote and it was two for one against and the last man abstained.

Rupert Ellis, (the bear) voted to go in early, as did the cook Joe ????

I voted to stay for the end, and Taffy, the mate never voted at all.

So the crew won the vote, but I said that we would have two more

hauls. The bear said that they had out voted me so why were we not going in early. I replied , well Taffy will shoot the gear, I will go to bed and you two will be sober for landing.

Fishing with the Ropes

That was 1988 and Rupert to this day still brings it up, but deep down he knew that I was right, when he asked Taffy why he did not vote, taffy replied that he had sailed with me for over 20 years and knew the outcome before they did.

Another incident was in 1981, when I owned a boat called Carmaran, I say owned, but I was £110,000.00 in debt to the office, after a major refit, they were not happy that I had decided to fish from N Shields, so after a few trips I had to go to GY on personal business.

While I was in GY, Danbrit fish sent a crew up to take the boat off me. But when they arrived they got a bit of a shock. As they were about to take over the boat, my crew told them, very politely to fuck off.

You expect a crew to stick by you at sea, but in dock they did not have to, but to be honest if I was one of the Grimsby lads no way would I have argued with those guys.

So thank you lads for sticking by me.

My crew were all Geordie lads . John Johnson/ Mad jonna

Keith Johnson/ Daft Jonna, and Keith Harvey. Let's put it this way I never shouted at them while at sea. a brilliant crew.

Another lad I must name is John Lewis, (little lewie) he had just finished on the deep water trawlers, it was late 70s and most of them had been scrapped or sold on. Anyway he was new to the ropes, I think it was only his third trip with me on the Ada Jean, (mothers name) we were three handed and on the very first day the mate Charlie Devine cut his hand ,very bad cut it was, so a boat from Blyth was on his way in and offered to take him ashore.

We had only shot two hauls, but there were 30 boxes of flatfish, and I was a bit weary about leaving the anchor spot, in the case of another boat arriving. After asking Lewie if he thought he could handle the job with just the two of us, he answered "only if you help".

We did just two hauls a day and after 10 days landed 160 kits of fish, on landing day he told me that he would NEVER have worked short handed on a trawler. RIP. Lewie. With a lot of the trawler lads starting with the ropes, I was amazed at how many of them struggled when it came to splicing two ropes together. Don't get me wrong most of them could do a splice in normal rope, but the rope we used was made extra tightly spun, so you had to use a spike to do the job, the rope they were used to could be done by hand.

When it came to mending nets trawler men were usually a lot faster as they did a lot of mending at sea, where as on the ropes we carried three or four spare nets. (our nets were about half the size of a trawl). So if we did have a big rip it was quicker to change nets, and the damaged one was mended by the net store, ashore. With the way our gear was shot, if we did hit an obstruction then 90% of the time it was the rope that got snagged, and not the net.

I told you earlier about Fred the whale, Ray Morse, and Ron Jensen, ok one day we were leaving the Humber river, the trainee was in the wheelhouse along with Taffy and myself, any way I said to Taffy that we were going to see Fred. Taffy then knew that we were going to the North East bank, for years Fred had been there in March, and April.

The trainee later asks Taffy who Fred was so Taffy told him that he was a whale. The lad then said that there is no way that I could know that we would see a whale. Three days later while heaving on the ropes, up pops Fred, well the lad was astounded, and I WAS RELIEVED. Thank you Fred, I wonder if he is still alive. If not RIP Fred.

Talking about different crew, I had a very strange chap sail with me in the Hatcliffe, and then the Bennison, he was with me for about three years, believe it or not I never knew his last name, we called him Banjo Joe, he was very well up on all the posh words. But to be honest he was as thick as shit.

In three years with me he never even tried to mend nets, splice ropes, or do anything else connected to fishing. So why keep him? Well he was on half share, (and happy with that). But tailing prawns, sorting through a mountain of weed to clear the fish, gutting fish, I have never seen anybody that could match his speed.

One day I told him that if he was to learn to mend and splice his wage would go up. He then told me that he would leave that to the real fishermen, and he was happy with the money that he was getting, very strange way to look at life but it takes all sorts. In the end I had to sack him as he had been over board three times. And the worry of his safety was getting to me.

Then on the other hand we had the type of men (NO NAMES) that knew it all, they had sailed with the best and made the biggest trips and spent most of their time telling the other lads what a crap skipper I was. Mostly when it came down to the graft they were crap.

This type of man never lasted long, not because I sacked them, but the lads were sick of the winging and they soon got the message that they could take their expertise on another boat, and leave us dumb boys to carry on. They were known in the fishing as Sea Lawyers.

One day in the mid 1970s, we arrived on the dock in GY all ready for sea. It was on the Ada Jean. One comical guy in the fleet had got a pot of paint. On the front of my wheelhouse, in red letters was a second name for my boat. THE MUPPIT SHOW. The lads were a bit annoyed at this, but I told them to leave it on, I said to them Kermit and his gang are very popular, so that means that we must be.

For the next year a few of the skippers named me Kermit.

Well thank you for that Billy West, and I still love it. I bet you do not know how I found out it was you Bill? And you never will.

Hey this is nice I have just typed three pager and no storms, or mishaps. See the job can be nice at times. I say NO mishaps?.

Joe going over board three times was not called that, it was part of his job.

Another dedicated crewman that I sailed with, Fred Sayers, we were fishing well, all big cod, we were working the tail end of the Dogger Bank. Freddy suffered from the curly rash. That is an allergy to the seaweed that was in that area. He came out in a bad rash, also his eyes were half closed. Like I said the fishing was Very good but I told him that we would move ground, away from the weed, his answer was, " Trev I cannot see very well but I can count" so he suffered for another two days, and we landed the best trip that I had got so far. To me that is a dedicated fisherman. RIP Freddy Sayers.

As I said earlier without the crew the skipper is redundant.

As most crew men that started there fishing life on the ropes knew the share basis, they worked in unison with the skipper. But when the deep sea trawlers went tits up, it took a lot of men a while to realise the difference between being on a wage, and being on a share of the catch.

To me if the trawler owners had given those men a better share of the catch, well put it this way they would have had more dedication and work from the men on the deck. And maybe they would have been easier to get to sea. But sadly the big trawler owners were too greedy to think of the men that they employed. I wish they were still with us, to read this. But to be honest did they give a shit?.

Talking about the crew, I remember when I was on the deck, aboard the Coral Bank with Mac the teacher one day we were hauling in the gear and Mac said to me, "Trev the forward rope will come tight, so go by the coil splices", and that I did, the rope came so tight that it was like an iron bar.

Normally the skipper would tell you to let go of the anchor, run along the rope and clear it. All Mac said was to stand clear and hope for the best. Well he then told me that the rope was in a patch of stones, he called it a shit or bust haul, if it pulled clear then the haul would be big, but 9 times out of 10 the rope parted, so no fish at all.

That night after dinner I said to Mac, "if it is so hard to pull over the stones, why bother with it"?. Well he says "the very few times I do get it home it always gives a bag of cod. Now to me one haul out of ten, well is it worth it?.

But he is the skipper so I kept my gob shut. Laid in my bunk that night I was thinking about the trawlers that used large bobbins to get over stony ground, the pair trawlers were now using a bobbin made from plastic so they were very light to handle on deck. With having holes in , when dropped over the rail they would then sink and so do the same job as the metal ones.

was how to be able to get it on and off.

As I said early on, if the I lay thinking about the rope pulling round stones on the sea bed and it came to me, why not have bobbins on the rope, the next problem ropes were stopped then most of the fish would swim free, anyway I must get some sleep so I will talk to the skipper in the morning about it. He is more cleverer than me, night night.

Next day I was telling Mac about my stupid idea, but he was very interested, and between us decided how it could be put into practice. After drawing out a few plans, he told me that when we docked he would get the engineers to construct a bobbin with a metal core, and the next trip we would give it a try. And this is the anchor rope bobbin mark one.

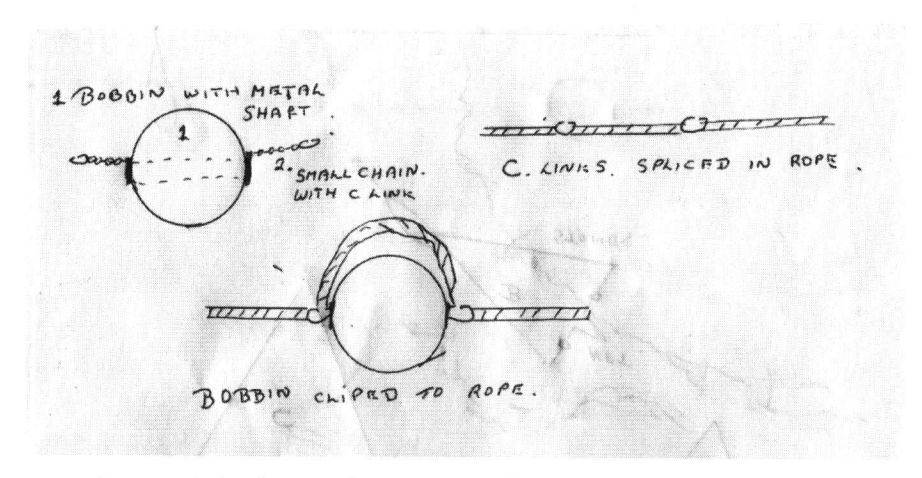

sorry about my lack of artistry but I cannot afford a design artist. As I said earlier I will stick to being a piss artist.

I hope you can see how the bobbin helped to get over the hard ground. It did work and after some body opened their gob, more than half the fleet were using this.

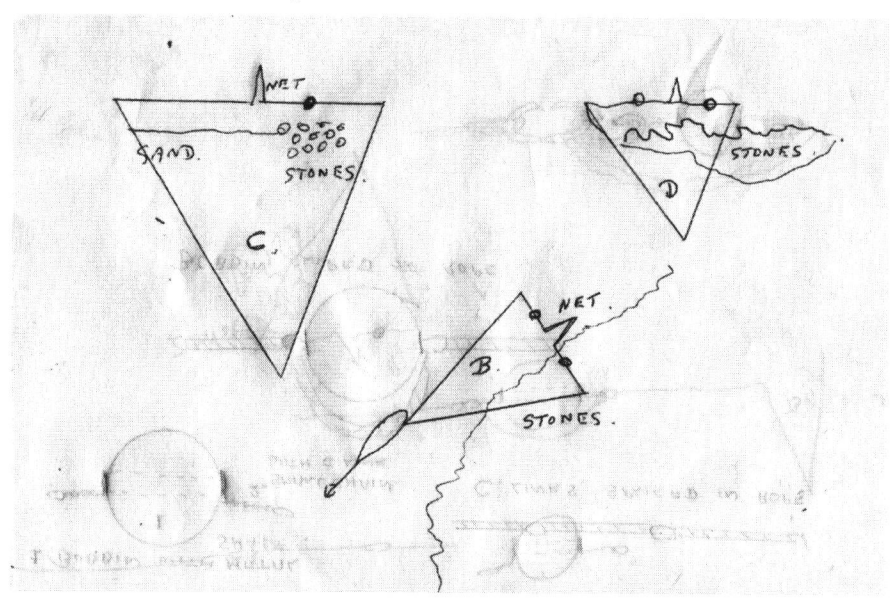

we should have patented it but there you go. A fly dragger with towing while heaving on the ropes, can get over hard ground as their ropes are not as slack as an anchor boat, so pulled through the hard ground easier.

As I am still on the chapter of the crew, I was chatting to one of my x crew men the other day, so as he had been on both types of rope fishing, he was the perfect man to tell me the difference. He was also one of the men that had no interest in the wheelhouse.

When I asked him why, he said that as long as he was earning a living why add to the worry. Mick Dalton was born in 1945, and started his fishing life with Alan Morse sn'r on the Conduan in 1970, and was on her for five years. He then went on to the Contester for two years with Alan Morse jn'r. I think he liked the name Alan.

In 1977 he then joined the Lindisfarn. The skipper was Jimmy Baily.

On asking Mick to tell me about any funny things that came to mind he told me that when he was on the Conduan, one of the other crew had a habit of smoking Mick's cigarettes. So he sat and emptied the tobacco out of one, replaced it with gunpowder. (out of one of the distress flares) by the way the other lad was called Peter Dixon.

Mick then put about half an inch of tobacco back in the end, when Peter woke up he asked Mick to pass him a ciggy, after a couple of drags WOOSH. Peter was in his bunk and his hair was on fire. Well he gave up smoking that day, and by the way Mick you are worse than me.

If you are squeamish do not read this next paragraph; well Peter had a very sweet tooth, every time he turned out he would grab a hand full of biscuits from the tin on the cabin table. The lads were saying that they were for all the crew, but there you go, they got their heads together and decided to stop him being so greedy. Well Mick after going to the toilet saved some of his waste, (sh★★) and put it in the biscuit tin. When Peter got out for hauling he put his hand in and got a few. Wow can you imagine. (you dirty bastards).

So now Peter is a non smoker and on a diet, I tell you what if I had known this when I gave Mickey the cooks job on the Bennison I would have promoted him to mate. And there is more to come.

On the Conduan one of the lads hung his sea boot socks up to dry, in the galley of all places, and as the boat was rolling one fell into the gravy pan, when Mickey left the deck to check on the dinner he just took it out, as the dinner was all ready instead of making new gravy he thought to himself, what the eye does not see.

When the crew sat down to dinner one of the crew asked him why he never had gravy on his?. Well Mickey said that he did not want any,

Fishing with the Ropes

as it was a bit salty, the skipper (old Alan) said that it did not taste salty, in fact it is very nice.

Luckily for the crew of the Conduan Mick left and joined the Contester.

On the Contester Mickey was talking to another of the crew, they were on about the danger of the job, especially the ropes, and getting tangled up when they were shooting. this lads name was Chris Kelly, well Mickey said that if ever he was going over the side, then he would take someone with him, strange lad.

Well one day It did happened Mickey got a bight of rope round his leg, he was being pulled over with the gear, and he grabbed hold of the power hauler. Chris was running to help but with luck the rope pulled clear. I think this is after shock, and relief but Chris said to Mickey "I was going to grab you, but remembered what you said about not going alone". Sadly a few years later Chris Kelly was killed while working on the deck, on a Spanish trawler. RIP Mate.

Now to carry on with the Contester, (Yes that is how we had to get on with life) after writing about the death of a good friend, I now move on to a funny bit.

One trip, steaming home on Contester a lad named Willy Jack decided to climb on to the top of the wheelhouse, so that when the trainee was leaving the wheelhouse the idea was to tip a barrel of water over him. But all clever ideas have there down side. While climbing up Willy fell and went overboard. Dopey sod.

Anyway the skipper shouted to Mickey "throw him a rope" and this he did, one small problem the rope was only three foot long. Now we have Willy in the water holding a small length of rope. After getting him back on board the skipper shouted to Mickey "what the fuck was the use of that?" Mickey replied "it was the nearest bit" to be honest he knew that Willy was a strong swimmer, also it was very fine weather.

One haul they got a very big haul, the deck was full, and the skipper young Alan Morse shouted down to one of the crew, (Peter Dixon), "come on lad get a move on" so Peter replied "who do you think I am, Billy Wiz?" well that did not go down well, back chatting the skipper, strangely Alan never said a word.

Trevor J Potter

On landing day, with a good shot of fish on the market, the skipper turned to Peter and said, "hey Billy wiz, pack you're gear and wiz off, and you are sacked". There you go, never backchat the skipper.

In 1977 Mickey Dolton left the Contester, and joined a boat called Lindisfarne, named after the island off the north east coast, or maybe the folk group I do not know, but they both have the same name so who cares. Not me.

The skipper was named Jimmy Bailey and when he gave Mickey a job, he did not know what he was in for. As I had known Jimmy I had to ask Mickey for his opinion of him as a skipper, his answer was that Jim was his best mate ashore, but at sea he hardly ever spoke to any of the crew. That is the fact of being a skipper, you could not get to close to the lads, especially on a boat with six crew men. He was not being ignorant, just being a skipper.

One haul the net came up full to the mouth with cod, they managed to get a few lifts onboard, (200 boxes) but then the net started to sink, all the air in the fish had gone and instead of the fish floating, they were now a dead weight. Jim shouted to Mickey "slack on the rope slowly" the rope was not long enough and they lost the rest of the fish, along with half of the net.

Steaming in to Shields with all the fish still to gut, Jimmy shouted down to his son Andy, he told him to stop standing about and get amongst them.

So he did, he went and sat in the middle of the haul, with no gutting knife, Jimmy shook his head and slammed the wheelhouse window shut. I believe Andy thought his dad wanted to take a photo. Well Andy was not the first in line when they were giving out the little grey cells. After landing and all the jobs done Andy said he was off to ring a taxi, so Mickey told him to get him one as well the reply was "sorry I have only got one 10p" HELP.

The next trip they were to be very lucky, they were fishing off the island of Helgoland, and doing very well it was flat calm and very hot, they caught a massive haul of small codling, it was that big they had to dump some of the fish, as the heat turned them into mush.

When the decks were clear the skipper shot another haul, it was also very good, so he decided to run into the island until the lads had put the

Fishing with the Ropes

fish away, with laying in the harbour the boat would not be rolling about, so less fish to dump.

The next morning ,after a good nights kip they sailed, Jimmy's idea was to have one more day and then steam home to Shields. On leaving the harbour the boat touched the bottom, now this is not normally a problem as it is very soft and no rocks to cause damage.

Mickey later went to the fish room to get some bacon off the ice, when he opened the hatch to his horror the fish room was full to the top with water Jimmy not wasting time got out a MAY-DAY.

It did not take the lifeboat from the island long to get to them, put powerful pumps on board and escort them back in when in safe harbour they sent a diver down and it was found that she had a damaged plank. That was patched up and the Lindisfarne went to Esberjerg and was put on the slip for new planking. It was later found out that he had not hit a sand bank, but an old wrecked submarine.

While on the slips the owners decided to have a shelter deck made and fitted, so to me out of every mishap something good can come out of it. Mickey left the Lindisfarn in 1983. in 1986 he decided to try anchor bashing. He joined a boat called the Bennison, and guess who the skipper was, yep yours truly.

Crew may solve boat mystery

EIGHT North Shields crewmen, who were rescued from their leaking fishing boat off the German coat, could today solve the mystery of their stricken vessel.

The agents and part owners of the 50-tonne seine netter Lindisfarne, Richard Irvin and Sons of North Shields, are waiting to hear what caused the ship's fish hold to half fill with water.

A spokesman said they expected the captain, James Bailey from North Shields, and his seven-man crew to be in contact some time today.

"We still have no idea what caused the leak, but at least we know they are all safe," he said

The dream began yesterday when the Lindisfarne started taking water during a four-day trip into the North Sea.

A distress cal was answered by the German coastguard at Bremen, and the rescue cruiser HERMANN Ritter and a helicopter were sent to the scene.

Another North Shields fishing boat the Bishop Burton stood by as the crew was taken off. The Lindisfarne was pumped out, and then towed to Germany.

The agents spokesman said it is not known when the men or their vessel would return to the Tyne.

"It all depends on what condition the boat is in. We don't know anything until they contact us," he said.

E.C. 9.12.83

Evening Chronicle.

Just think if the weather conditions had not been so good, this could be a completely different story.

LINDISFARNE

When I asked Dinky what he thought of the difference from fly shooting to anchor bashing, he said that on the fly draggers they would shoot an average of 8 hauls per day.

On the anchor he was shocked that I only shot 4 per day. But my boat only had 4 crewmen, and a fly dragger had 8. plus you can not rush flat fishing. There I go repeating myself. To be honest I think that Dinky thought I was a lazy sod.

Also have you noticed his name has changed from Mickey to Dinky. Well that is because he is a shortarsed lad.

As I got to know him better, I found that if he was moaning and groaning he was happy, but if he went silent then somebody had upset him, usually it would be me, as it became a hobby of mine.

All in all he is a great shipmate, and a very good cook. When he was telling me about the difference between the two type's of fishing he also commented on the fact that if Jimmy Bailey said they were sailing at 8am, they did, his first trip with me I told the lads to be down for sailing at 8am and he was shocked at the fact that we sailed at midnight. DINKY DALTON sailed with me 3 years.

Chapter 11 - Egon Thomson

At the beginning of this book I told you how the Danish fishermen came over to the UK, during the Second World War. But not all of them did, some decided to stay at home and fish. The problem they had, was that they were under very strict rules, laid down by the occupying German forces. One such man was Egons father, Svend Stisen Thomsen. the boat was named the Alladin.

He was one of the men that decided to stay, but was told that he could not go further out than 50 miles from the coast, this was later extended to 90 miles due to lack of fish. Once at sea, like all fishermen he followed the fish, not the rules.

At the time the British told all occupied fishermen to sail for English ports, only 40 to 50 boats did. The fishermen also had all their radio's taken off the boats. It must have been very hard for them, as if they were seen outside the 90 mile limit the Germans shot at them and even dropped bombs on them, as they took it that they were trying to escape to the UK. If that was not bad enough the English would bomb them, thinking they were spying.

Egons father told him that in September 1939 there were about 100 anchor boats fishing in the German Bight and Helgoland, during the night when the boats do not fish the Germans laid a massive minefield around their coast. Sadly they did not tell the fishermen.

The next day the first of many boats was blown up, she was the NORDSTRAND, and none of the four crewmen was found alive. Later four anchor boats were lost on the same day, they were fishing about 20 miles outside the limit, and the weather was fine, they were

Fishing with the Ropes

presumed sunk by German submarines. They were the Danish boats, E-J-JAM/ GERLIS/ MERCATOR/ and POLARIS.

The next day another boat the L,WULFF, E40, was boarded by a German sub crew, after showing her papers that told them they had just sailed from Holland, they were allowed to carry on with the trip, sadly the same day the WULFF came across a lot of wreckage, they also found Father and son ,lashed together and tied to an anchor buoy, they were both dead. It was later found out that the 4 anchor boats that were sunk had landed their fish in Grimsby the previous trip.

As fishing with ropes they knew the mine fields well, the Germans, worried that they were passing on info to the British, said that any boat landing fish into the UK would be sunk.

Well Egon wanted to go fishing, but his father was not happy with this, especially as it was war time. It is hard enough in normal fishing, but with the mines and bombing from both sides, well it was asking for trouble. But he did relent, and at the age of 16 Egon got a job on a brand new boat, but while it was getting fitted out he did do one trip with his father on the Aladdin. His father said that it was unlucky for family to sail together in wartime. (I have never believed in family sailing together at any time).

Well he signed on as cook, on 4 % of the catch, after expenses. He also told me that all the fishing boats were on a strict amount of fuel they were allowed enough to do seven days a month.

That trip they fished outside the limit, as they had too most trips. They dropped the anchor as it was getting dark, so would not start fishing until the next morning. When they did get up to flat calm weather Egon got the shock of his young life. Floating about five yards off the boat there was a large horned mine. (fuck that, I would have left fishing there and then.) anyway no damage as it did pass safely. But I bet they had one eye on the water after seeing that.

After 4 days fishing they had a very big trip of flatfish, and decided to go home, before taking the anchor they cleared the deck of fish, it was now dark and Egon told me that, they had all the deck lights on all of a sudden an airplane swooped down, it did not shoot at them, but they did get off the deck as fast as they could.

The fact is that the allies were not happy about the boats from Denmark fishing to feed the German troops. The Danes did have a choice at the start of the war, to sail to England, but if you have a family, would you leave them?. Well I would not have. When they landed that trip he told me that his wage came to 1200 Kroner, do not ask, but it was a very large sum of money for a young lad.

He then joined the new boat with Oscar Veno. He was to stay with this man for a very long time, and do very well. Hey folks I have that much info off Egon about the wartime fishing, I think that I could write a book on it. But to be honest I want to move to the year that he and two other Danish fishermen came over to England in 1952.

One thing I must tell you about is a Danish boat came across two life rafts, tied together, in them were 9 German air men. The fishing boat, (E264, HARMONEY) Sent up a distress rocket, and a German gunboat came out and took them ashore.

It worked both ways, as the same boat a month later picked up two British airmen, but had to take them home to Esbejerg. So prisoners of war, but they were alive. Another thing, in the last year of the war a lot of Danish resistance men were being hunted down by the Germans, and by then most of the fleet knew the outcome of the war was very close. So the fishing boats started to bring the freedom fighters to England. Egon is very proud of the fact that his father was one of those skippers. I would like to speak for my self now.

A BIG THANK YOU TO ALL the Danish fishermen that helped us.

Another thing that Egon did not know at the time, his father had started to help the resistance fighters. he would go out to sea, meet up with another anchor boat and load up with canisters of guns and ammo.

One trip he was to meet a boat on the Dogger Bank. he arrived late but was laid at anchor and flashing a light to attract the boat he was to get the supplies off.(the Kvik), while he was flashing the light he was attacked by a war plane.(nation unknown) he then turned all his lights off, and steamed to Grimsby.

Arriving at Grimsby he saw the boat that he was to meet on the bank, the Kvik, for some reason had not sailed. His father was taken down to London, they ask him to load up the canisters in GY. And then do a trip fishing, as the fish and ice would be put on top of the dodgy cargo.

Fishing with the Ropes

Well he told the ministry that it would be too risky, as if a boat had been to England and landed, on arrival back in Denmark the boat would be searched from stem to stern, and he and his crew would be shot.

Any way the war is now over so in January 1956 Egon and two other fishermen decided to come over to Grimsby, I think they were needed to show us dopey English How to FISH WITH ROPES. The other two men were Leif Gravesen and Arge Lund. At that time the three of them never dreamed that they were to become VERY successful skipper owners.

Egon is the same as I was two or three trips and then have some time ashore, before joining another boat, you could only carry on like that if you were single, to me enjoy life while you are young. Also you never knew if the next trip was your last. Like in 1959 an anchor boat, KYANA, was lost with all hands, it was owned by another skipper, Volmer Nielsen. So that is why most fishermen made sure that they enjoyed their time ashore.

Maybe some of the people that looked down their noses at us lads enjoying life should have done a trip with us. Egon sailed on a few boats before he got to start as skipper, all of them were GY boats and all had Danish skippers, it was not until the late 50s and early 60s that the English lads started to take an anchor boat away skipper.

The first one was Len Collings. Danbrit, as I have said before anchor bashing is a fine art, and it took a long time to learn the ropes, excuse the pun, . when Egon was cook on a boat called the Dorny, with Peter Nyborg on the third day at sea he got up in the morning and could not get his boots on, his foot was swelled up and he was in agony. Being early in the trip Peter put him onboard another boat that was homeward bound, the Emmy.

When he got home to GY. He was told that he had gout. (piss off Egon only the rich get that,) he was ashore for three month, before being passed fit for sea. He then signed on a boat called CREAG MHOR, skipper Tage Larsen, as it was getting on in the year he only did one trip. Tage was to go to the Moray Firth for the winter, but Egon said it was to cold, (SOFT SOD). I am now going to quote from Egons letter to me, word for word. And the reason is, can you remember a few pages back. I told you that the people ashore used to look down on us fishermen?.

My time ashore was spent mostly going round drinking, around Freeman street pubs, there was always somebody that just landed, and the bars were full of fishermen, both English and foreign. Plenty of female company, we had a saying at sea, no fish, no money, no money no woman. So we worked hard, day and night to make sure we had the money, that was life as a fisherman, work hard play hard, up to 28 days at sea, and only the same three faces to look at.

So when we were ashore we let ourselves go, I know it gave fishermen a bad name, but we are only human after all.

I then joined a boat called the Des, the skipper was Ejner Eskeson. Leif Gravesen was deck hand and the cook was a man called Poul, another Danish lad. (hey my spell checker is going mad, with all this Danish).

Any way that is why we were called weekend millionars.in1959 Egon started his skippers career, he took a boat called Well Bank, it was November so most anchor boats were on their last trip. He went to a fishing ground off the Danish coast, with no luck, he told me that he was scratching around for 18 days. Then he struck gold. (or should I say silver) as he started to fish very well with large haddock. After two days he had turned a bad trip into a very good one.

On the second night he was laid in his bunk, it was only 8PM but with it being winter, and the fact he was well North the daylight hours were very short. The weather changed from decent to a full storm, in one hour. He remembers well that at 9 PM they were hit by a massive wave. The wheel house windows caved in, and he was trying to get out of his bunk, but the amount of water held him back, when it did clear he found that the starboard door had gone, also a couple of the wheelhouse windows. Talk about a cold shower in the mornings, but seriously when he put the deck lights on, he got a big shock, all the starboard rail was gone, the net and the platform it was lashed to was also gone. And not one single thing was left on the deck.

The most amazing thing is the anchor gear held. Egon tells me that if the boat had not been so strong, then he would have lost her.

After the deck was clear of water he went to the cabin, forward, and to his amazement it was dry. They then checked the engine room and that was also dry. They did have a bit of a job starting the engine, as a lot of water had gone down the exhaust.

Fishing with the Ropes

With luck as fast as the storm had hit them, it only lasted 4 hours, how mad is that, by one am it was calm. With all the damage he had to go home, there was another boat 3 miles off, the Martin Norman, she had suffered no damage at all. Funny thing weather?. His crew were Cliff Clasper, and the owners son Eric Nielsen.

Young Eric a lad I knew well went on to skipper the boat for the remainder of his life at sea.

Also I know how lucky they were to be on such a strong boat, as I sailed in her sister ship East Bank, they were both built on the Humber river, and the yarn goes that the shipyard that built them went bankrupt.

Reason, well they put that much wood into them ,it ended up costing more than the quoted price. Where a Scottish, or Danish boat was built with every second rib only going just below the deck, this shipyard made every rib down to the keel.

Brilliant, safe, but very expensive. But by god they were the two strongest wooden boats in the UK. Looking at this next picture, I think that is why Egon and his crew are still with us. I do know that the Well Bank was still fishing after I retired from the sea.

The funny part of this is that young Erik Nielsen had to have two inches cut off her stem, because of new EU rules, how mad is that, after all those years at sea, and all the weather she had put away, some prick in another country said she was too long, for his ticket.

Trevor J Potter

SOLID
AFT
END
LIFTED →

RAIL
COMPNEATLY
GONE.

WELL BANK SHOWING STORM DAMMAGE.

As I said not many boats could have taken that wave and survived.

Between 1967 and 1970 Egon was skipper of a boat called the JERSEY, one day he was sat in the house listening to the boats at sea, (we all had radios with the shipping bands on). Even when we were ashore we kept up with what was going on out at the fishing grounds.

One of the skippers Jens Thomsen, on a boat the SHEARBILL, was asking the office to send out a part for the main engine, as they could not get it started. She belonged to a firm called Franklins. Egon rang the office and told them to put the part on board the Jersey.

He was ready for sea but the weather forecast was very bad, normally s skipper would let the storm pass before sailing, but with the other boat having no engine Egon sailed on the next tide. Steaming down the Humber river he passed another boat going in, she was the Denston, skipper Richard Johansen. Richard called him on the VHF, and asked Egon if he knew that there was a bad storm on the way. When told about the Sherbill 120 mile off and no power, all Richard said was "good on you mate safe trip".

He did deliver the part, and within 3 hours they had the engine running. Both boats spent three days riding out the storm, as Egon said, "one day I might be me in a tight spot".

Fishing with the Ropes

That is how 99% of fishermen thought, thank god. He was then offered a brand new boat, a firm called Tom Sleights ,(the largest anchor boat firm in GY) was run by a man named Charlie Procter, and he was no mug. The boat was the Grena Dawn, they sailed in early February, and landed 300 kit of large cod, for £1200.00.

Returning to the same spot, the next trip, the fish had moved, or been landed in GY. Moving around and plodding away for the next 10 days, he got a call over the radio that he was now a dad, his girlfriend Rena had given him a son 25, feb,1959, congrats to you both, a bit late I know as that was 53 years ago. Back to the trip, after 14 days scratching around, he then tried the south west patch, a very shallow and dangerous spot to be on, especially that time of year. The fishing was good (large flatfish).I said earlier that the ropes did not work well in the dark, and that is true, but with a full moon, and the shallow water, and things Egon had picked up over the years, he did fish all night and was catching the same amount. You kept that one quiet you crafty old sod.

He had a very good year in the Grena Dawn, but his next year was a struggle , as it was with most of the fleet. One trip Egon suffered a very bad asthma attack, and they had to go home. The doctors told him it was caused by his living conditions, as on most anchor boats the whole crew slept in a very small cabin, with a coal fire.

Not many anchor boats had a cabin behind the wheelhouse, but in the 60s onwards all the new boats were built bigger, and with better accommodation. All had a larger wheelhouse, so room for the skipper to have his own cabin. It was not to be posh, but the fact that the radio could be moved out of the forward cabin, and the skipper living in the wheelhouse, he was better aware of any mishaps.

Even the old boats that used to have small sheds were slowly being updated. Egon carried on but with the boats getting bigger, he now needed a ticket to take a boat to sea, as there were many x trawler men walking around with skippers tickets he had no problem getting one to sign on as the skipper, and Egon was called the fishing instructor.

A man using his ticket got 1% extra, sadly a few of them started to think they were in charge, and by law they were. So Egon decided to get his own ticket, but first he had to get British citizenship, and that he did. After getting his ticket he moved to Arcona fishing co.

The boat he took was Arcona Champion, he had her for one year, the office then asked him if he was interested in taking another boat, but he was to travel to Denmark and buy one, it would be his choice of boat, well he was not keen on leaving the Champion, but was told he would be given a share of ownership.

He could not turn that down so off he went. The top price he was given was £12000.00, so he bought a boat for that amount. She was renamed Arcona Bay.

He was to spend the rest of his fishing life in her, and did very well. In 1987 with fishing getting harder, with all the EU rules he decided to retire. Arcona Bay was sold to Fleetwood for £56000.00. if he had sold her two years earlier he would have got £85000.00.that's life.

EGON THOMSEN

THE English fishing industry owes a lot to this man and many more Danish fishermen. Thank you to all, we learnt a lot.

Fishing with the Ropes

EGON THOMSEN AND AUGA LUND ON GRENA DAWN

JERSEY. 1965 TO 1969.

Chapter 12 - Allsorts

Why is this chapter called allsorts? Well that is what it is, I am waiting to catch another fisherman to talk to, so I will drivel on about things that may or may not interest you. One big difference from the big trawlers and the rope boats was the food. On trawlers, as the crew was on a wage the firm had to pay for the food stores. And to be honest, as I have sailed on them you get better fed in hospital.

On the anchor boats the crew paid for their own stores, so on most of them the food was top class, strange as it may seem we still had a fish meal every second night. And that was my favourite meal, also most other men agreed with me. This may sound daft to you but on most boats the cook would buy a box of smoked haddock, and make a fish soup for the first day, (it was good for the stomach, and the hangover).

Imagine that, a fishing boat buying fish to take to sea, told you we had to be mad, or at least it helped if you were. Hey would you all like the recipe?. ok then start with a 2 or 3 gallon pan, peel a dollop of spuds, then boil them for one hour, add ten fillets of smoked haddock, throw in half a dozen onions, loads of salt and pepper, boil full power for an hour or so, add 1 or 2 tins of milk, any brand will do, then simmer until you have eaten it all. By the way you can make a smaller one, but with 4 men we had to make sure it lasted about 2 days. I highly recommend it. Sorry I forgot some boats added a pack of Lurpak butter.

Another little trick to save time was that the cook would put the spuds in a fish basket, with a shovel of coal, tow it from the stem of the boat, the bow wave would bounce them about and after shooting the ropes the spuds would come up skinless. So if you hate peeling spuds,

Fishing with the Ropes

buy a boat. But beware, the odd cook thinks it is better to tow them aft side, so the propeller wash would clean them faster. But if the skipper goes astern the spuds will end up in the propeller. So mashed tatty for dinner.

The cook also washed the galley and cabin mats the same way and that was ok by me, until one day I went astern while picking the anchor up and the engine stopped. I thought we had picked up some floating net or rope, so when I looked over the stern I saw that it was the cabin mat. Normally no problem, as they were only coconut matting. But??? Instead of towing it on a light rope, he used leaded fishing rope. It was a bit embarrassing when I had to ask another boat to tow it clear. NO I AM NOT going to name him.

Another time, when I was mate on the Coral Bank, with Mac, we were plodding away on 3 or 4 baskets of flatfish. It was flat calm and very hot, Mac always shot very long slow hauls so plenty of time off, after putting the fish away I looked for the flag on the anchor gear and saw that we still had about half an hour or more before we were to start hauling.

After making him a pot of tea I went down the cabin, more to get out of the sun than anything.(I hate the sun, give me snow any day). Well I dozed off, when I woke up I saw that I had been asleep for well over an hour. STRANGE. I went up on deck and as I was leaving the hatch I saw the anchor gear about a mile astern of us.

I found Mac sat on the wheelhouse step, fast asleep? Aw come on it was hot, I woke him and asked if we were at the anchor yet. To his embarrassment we had passed it. Well I had to laugh, even though I knew the haul was fucked. When we did clip up to the anchor, instead of both ropes leading aft, we had one leading forward. That meant that the net was now under the boat.

Sorry Mac it had to come out one day.

Trevor J Potter

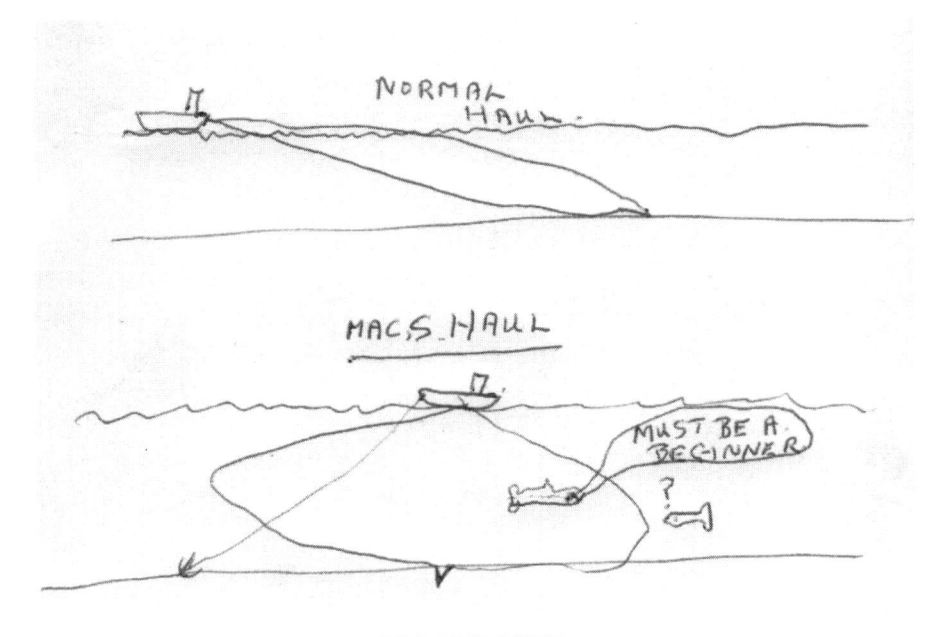

NORMAL HAUL

MACS HAUL

MUST BE A BEGINNER?

SORRY MATE.

As I am on about fishing with ropes, I got a shock when I visited three fishing heritage centres in the UK, all were very good but sadly EVEN they had focused on herring drifters and the trawlers, the first I will forgive, as they never had a rope fishing boat out of the harbour, and that was LOWESTOFT, the next one was Aberdeen, again herring, trawling, and oil rigs, but very little info on fly shooting. The last one was a shock, it was the Grimsby Fishing centre.

Out of the three I would say the GY one was the best, except for one MAJOR down. And that was even though Grimsby had the biggest fleet of anchor boats in the UK, (almost 200 boats in the early 70s) they still concentrated on trawling. If you think of the fact that from 1975 onwards the trawler fleet was all but gone. GY was kept going for another 10 years by the small wooden fleet.

Another strange thing that amazes me, is that when I sent this book to the history press, it was turned down. They told me that the fishing subject had been covered. Well all I can do is say sorry to all the Danish men that gave us a cheap environment friendly way of fishing. Even though us English had to show you how to make a decent coiler. Then the Danish went one better and came up with the rope reels.

Fishing with the Ropes

The first boat that had the rope reels fitted in Grimsby was called the LOCHERN she was launched in Denmark. Skipper Barry Emerson, and on her maiden trip broke the port record. £8000.00. so even though the lads did not have to drag ropes away, they were kept busy gutting.

As I said before, the use of reels on rope boats saved a lot of lives, also a lot of broken limbs. I personally was not to keen on getting them fitted, as the more machinery you have, the more things to go wrong. In 1976 my partner Tony Chester said it was time to move on and get them. Well out of about 160 anchor boats there was only two without the reels. The Island, (Ada Jean), and the Obelisk. I wanted to be the last one but I knew that Alex would not budge.

There were 3 firms in Denmark making them, and one in Scotland, most of the fly draggers had the Lossie reels fitted, with great success. The one or two anchor boats that tried them, for some reason they did not work well. With hydraulics making a big impact on the fishing boats, we then went on to net haulers, (power blocks) the winch was next, (no more winch belts to change) and on a few boats they even fitted hydraulic pumps on to the deck bilge pumps.

Where is it going to end?. Hydraulic crew maybe.

Trevor J Potter

Elliott & Garrood L^td.

INGATE IRONWORKS
BECCLES, SUFFOLK
Telephone: Beccles 2277

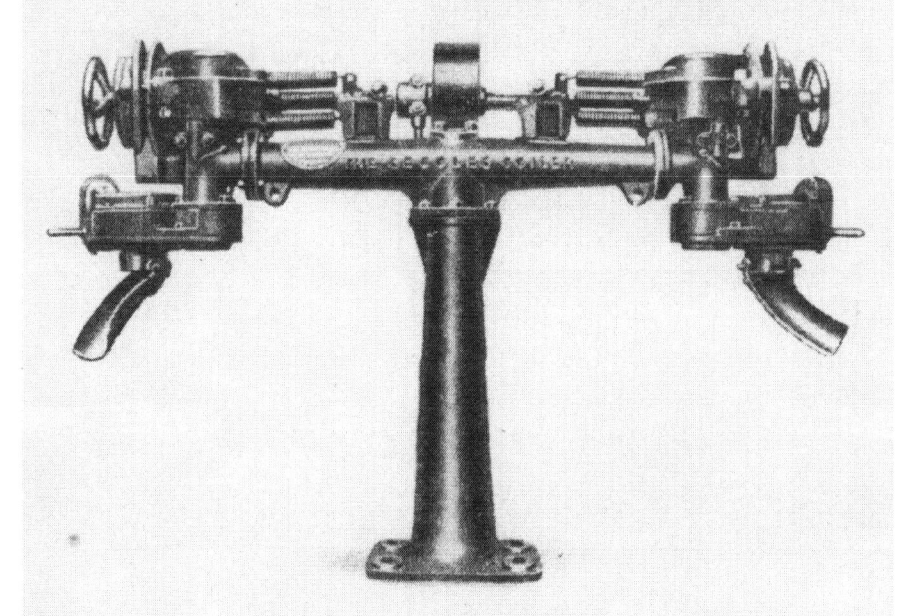

THE UNRIVALLED BECCLES ROPE COILER

EFFICIENT, STURDY and DEPENDABLE

Spare Parts obtainable from stock and from Agents along the East Coast

SEINE WINCHES — -TRAWL WINCHES

THE INFAMOUS BECCLES COILER *If I had known what they were making in that factory when I was at school, I would have blown it up. Not really as that is now two good fishing things that came from Beccles.*

O did I not tell you ? I was born there. Sorry.

Chapter 13 - Cliff Ellis

So where do I start with this man? One of the top earners with the ropes in the UK, but he did not want to talk to me?. Not because he is big headed, just the opposite, I would say very shy.

When he did chat, he said to me that his memory had gone, but I know different. He did tell me that all he did was his own thing, and that was catch fish. Cliff was born in Grimsby in 1936, and started going to sea at the age of 15, on the deep water trawlers. He only did one year, then moved to the anchor boats, his first boat was called the Roda.

Then he was called up to do his national service, I am glad that I was to young for that lark. well Cliff spent three years in the army, with being a fisherman, they normally put you in the Navy, but who am I to cause waves.

On finishing his national service he went back hone to Grimsby and joined another anchor boat. The Straymoy, with Julian Egon, and then the Macata with Evald Hansen. Note the Danish names.

I then asked him how he came to fish from North Shields, he smiled and said "the cod war" so maybe he had enough of the army life. Or just wanted a quiet life. A QUIET LIFE IN NORTH SHIELDS?, well whatever.1956 Cliff joined the Contester, with Norry Morse.

Well it had to be a Con boat and a Morse as skipper. In 1958 he sat for his skippers ticket. And the first boat he was given was the Contester. And after that the Conmoran. Cliff did very well in both boats, fly shooting.

Richard Irvins, the office that ran all the Ben boats, (deep water trawlers,) and were agents for the Morse family, not being slow, saw the potential that Cliff had as a big earner. And so had a fly dragger built. That was the Lindisfarne, and to get Cliff interested they gave him a share in her. Mind you he did tell me that it was not a great deal, but what do we expect from a trawler owner.

He said not great, but it was enough to make him move, plus there was no way the Morse family was going to build him a brand new boat. (daft sods). So in July 1972 Cliff took over the Queen of the fleet. Cliff had a name for being very strict at sea, but also if you did your job he was a very fair man, and a gent to sail with.

But you always knew who the boss was, I was also told that when the fishing was slack Cliff was VERY quiet, well you must think of the pressure that he was under, it is not easy being the top earner. When he was on fish the music would come on the deck and the skipper started to laugh and joke with the lads. You would think that is normal, but I was the opposite, if I was not catching fish then I used to laugh and joke. when I did find the fish I went very quiet, I started to worry about keeping among them. But who said I was normal, not me.

The Lindisfarne was also the first boat on the east coast of England to try out a new gadget, a warp tension meter. That was a new gadget that told the skipper if he was fast on a wreck? No seriously it would tell the skipper that one rope was harder than the other. It was his job to decide if the rope was meant to have more tension than the other one.

I was speaking to cliff today 2012, and he said that it was a great help, that surprised me, as I thought that it would only be of help to a trawler. He then told me that with the meters in the wheelhouse he could keep the gear level without even looking at it. Remember Ron Jensen stood in between the ropes, pressing them down.

Seiner's meter

F.N. 25-X-14

THE TOP North Shields seiner, *Lindisfarne*, sailed for the grounds at the weekend equipped with a warp tension meter.

D.E.V. Engineering of Wallsend on Tyne is developing small-boat warp tension meters and this is the firm's first installation.

The tension meter is being used while seine netting, but will be modified for when the 50-ton *Lindisfarne* goes trawling. The engineering firm plans to produce the meters for sale when developed.

D.E.V. Engineering has been working closely with Skipper Cliff Ellis of *Lindisfarne*, who is confident the unit will be a success after some months on the project.

The design of the units is based on that being used and developed in Australia and New Zealand described by John Burgess last week.

from the fishing news 1974.

I did say where is it going to end, well the E.U. sorted that one out for us. To be honest I thought it was to screw on to the skippers head to tell if he was under any tension, with the lads on the deck. Or the bank manager or the wife or the fact that there was not enough fish. well you live and learn.

In 1976 after five great years in Lindisfarne, cliff was offered another deal. And that was to go into part ownership of a new steel boat, that was to be built for the ropes and trawling. The mans name was Valma Nielsen, he owned a few anchor boats in Grimsby.

Now with Cliff onboard he was about to branch out, into fly dragging. Here is the new boat.

CHRISTINE NIELSEN.

She was later fitted with a full shelter deck, and the crew were then fully protected from the weather. And also the most important fact, she would now be able to fish in bad weather.

Cliff kept the Nielsen until he retired in 2000, he made lots of money, for lots of people, and in 1988 he was awarded the British Empire Medal. But like he said to me. "I was just doing my own thing". "trying to earn a living".

Well Cliff Ellis you certainly did that.

Fishing with the Ropes

● Mr Clifford Ellis after receiving his British Empire Medal.
Picture: PAUL DODDS

Two receive British Empire Medals

TWO Tyneside men featured in the Queens Birthday Honours list were presented with their British Empire Medals yesterday.

Mr Lawrence Gray, 49, of Garth 24 Killingworth, and Mr Clifford Ellis, 52, of Linskill Terace, North Shields, received their medals in separate ceremonies from the Lord Lieutenant of Tyne Wear, Sir Ralph Carr-Ellison.

In the first ceremony at Swan Hunter shipyard in Wallsend Mr Gray received his medal, awarded for his services to first aid.

Mr Gray, a joiner, has been a member of the yard's first aid corps for 29 years and chairman for the last 16 years.

He is a member of the Association of St John Ambulance and the Northumbrian Guild of Casualties, who act the part of disaster victims in emergency services training exercises.

Mr Gray also teaches first aid and has won many first aid competition trophies for the yard.

He was nominated for his medal by the yard management and said he was very proud of the award, which was not only his but also a tribute to his colleagues.

The second presentation took place at Wallsend Town Hall, where Mr Ellis received his medal for services to North-East fishing.

Mr Ellis is skipper and part-owner of the Christine Nielsen, which has been the top performing vessel in North Shields for a number of years.

He has been a fisherman since the age of 15 and was nominated for his award by the Ministry of Agriculture, Fisheries and Food.

Chapter 14 - Back To The Lads

I was talking to an old friend of mine the other day, he is from Hartlepool, Dicky Leighton, and he now runs the pub on North Shields fish quay, The New Dolphin. If you are ever in Shields you should try it. OK the advert is over, on with his yarn. Dicky was born in Hartlepool in 1948 and started sea on an anchor boat called the Clavis, with Jimmy Thane, his second year was on the Tarma with Kenny Green. I know that they mean nothing to you but it is nice to remember the old guys. Kenny Green owned the Tarma but landed in GY all the time.

Anyway Dicky told me that his first visit to Shields was on his 18th birthday in a boat called Straymoy, they were on the way up to the Moray Firth for the winter fishing. That was the same year that I was up in the Firth, strange I never met him. Mind you it was night fishing and you could not see very far. We did not get to know each other until 1978, when he was a great help to me, with the prawn trawling lark.

Anyway Dicky, (when he was 18) then decided to try fishing from Esbejerg, Denmark he spent two years on a boat called the Nicolina, with a skipper named Berga Andersen. That is until the skipper and his father, who owned the boat, had a fall out.

Berga told the crew that they were to go fishing and land in different ports in the UK. Everything they caught was sold for cash, and not one penny for the boat, now that to me sounds like a great job. After two or three landings they were arrested, so that was the end of the party.

Fishing with the Ropes

The crew were lucky as they were just following their skippers orders. So wisely Dicky decided to stay in England. After a couple of trips out of GY, sailing on a boat with Frankie Josefson, they landed in North shields, where Dicky decided to stay.

Bet you cannot name the boat that he joined? Or at least the first three letters of her name?. It is now 1969 and Yes it was one of the Con boats. Condowan to be exact. In 1972 Dicky was asked to go over to Denmark with a crew to bring back an anchor boat, she was called the LIL!GIT. on the trip home to Shields they were hit by a very bad storm. One of the crew told him that there was a small leak in the cabin, so he went to check it out. To his shock the small leak was now a big one, the cabin was full to overflowing.

Now an anchor boat will stay afloat with one compartment full but if the bulkhead (wall) to the fish room did not hold then there was no chance. With her being an elderly boat it did not hold for long.

So our Dicky is now skipper of an inflatable life raft, and with the boat going down so fast nobody knew of his new command. They were in the raft for 56 hours before they were spotted by a Russian factory trawler. Now I am not a lover of Russian cigarettes but I bet them lads were ready for one. After that Dicky decided to become an inshore fisherman. And ended up a very successful one.

Hey I know this has nothing to do with rope fishing, but when you read a book does it not do your head in when they take a whole page to say two lines?.

★★★

This short rotund man was stood in the cabin, he had deep piercing blue eyes when he looked at you it made you wonder what he was thinking. His jet black hair was combed back, with a quiff like a teddy boy from the sixties. He took out his tobacco tin and with life long expertise of rolling his own cigarettes by hand he made it look like a factory made one. Going on to the deck for some air he opened the watertight door, that was sadly in kneed of a repaint, as it was blistering and rust streaked from the years of wind and water.

When he arrived on the deck the wind was blowing that hard, the wavelets were being picked up by the wind and you would have thought that it was raining. But no there was a cloudless sky. And a wintry, watery sun shining down on to him. He then turned his back to the wind and relit his cigarette with his Zippo lighter. The quiff was now gone from his hair.

★★★

MY WAY.

This short fat lad made a fag, then went on the deck through a rusty door, it was sunny but blowing like f★★k, so he got soaked. He had to relight his tab twice. So why the f★★k did he not stay inside.

★★★

maybe I am just a lazy sod. And hate to waste ink???. Any way each to their own. Also the amount that they charge per page to print the book, well why waste money.

Hey all I will either have to leave the lager alone, or do my typing in the mornings. The next lad I spoke to had sailed with Cliff Ellis for a lot of years. Here are some of his tales, I have mentioned him before. Willy Jack, the one Dinky threw the rope to save his life.

Hey this is great, today I went down to the RNMDSF, for our weekly get together, popped into the dolphin for a swift pint and met an old friend , Johnny Goldsboro he was asking me if I remembered a lad called Alex Latimer, and I did, a right character, well John asked if I remember the time that Alex went fishing in the main street of North Shields. What he did was got some fresh fish off the market one morning, took it in a bag up to Bedford street, got himself a short cane tied twine to it and a bent nail on the end. He then opened a manhole cover, put one of his fish on the hook and lowered it down.

Every now and again as people were passing, he pulled up the fish and added it to his bag. It was that funny that the prank even went into the Shields weekly news. Along with a photo of him holding up one of his catch. Mad or what?.

Sorry back to Willy Jack, sorry for butting in Willy but if I did not write it down I would have forgot. Alex I mean.

Willy started life on the Icelandic trawlers, but in 1968 he decided to try the ropes, so he signed on the Contester with Cliff Ellis as all new hands on the ropes you had to start at the bottom, and that was cook.

Well he told me that he did not know how to fry an egg, but there you go. The other lads were Terry Fairly and Jimmy Bailey, and Fen

Fishing with the Ropes

Mundy snr. He did tell the lads that he had never been cook before, but they said to him not to worry, as the rope boats were not like trawlers. In other words you did not have to make bread or puddings.

On his first trip they told him to make porridge for the first haul, (3am) and a fry up for the second haul, well his first attempt at porridge was a disaster, Willy worried that it was not thick enough, he was told by one of the lads to put more in, so he did and more and more.

On picking up the dahn Willy had to watch the first two or three coil of rope, while the lads sat down to eat, by this time the porridge had been simmering away and thickening. I say thickening it was now a pan full of solid whatever. But being new they let him off, and had a sandwich.

As the years went by Willy became a great cook, he could now make dumplings, suet puddings, and a full Sunday roast, so what does Cliff do, get a new boat with a special oven, that defrosted and cooked separate meals. So all that learning from Willy has gone to waste.

That is what he first thought? Bang the frozen meals in, sit back and read a book. WRONG. As the dinners defrosted, and with the boat rolling about well they all spilt over, got mixed together and set fire. So funny full of smoke and nothing to cook in.

When they landed the new posh cooker was ripped out and replaced with a normal one. Good job you can now cook Willy.

Now Willy will admit this himself, in those days he was a bit of a piss artist, he had been sacked twice for missing the boat. But Cliff always took him back. I have said it before and will say it again, sober them up and you have the best crew that you could wish for.

But only so many times, and he was on his last chance. His boat the Lindisfarne landed every week and sailed the same day, they then had every second weekend ashore. So on their first landing of the trip Willy went for a few pints with one of the crew, his name Sandy Lyons, better known in the fleet as TIGER.

Anyway Willy says to him "I cannot get drunk as I am on my last warning" and Tiger told him not to worry as he would get him up for sailing, 4AM. So off they go to the Cresta club and had a few more, (I have sailed with Sandy, do not try to drink with him). Come 3 AM Sandy arrives at Willies house, and was told by his wife that there was no chance of getting him up.

Sandy said "leave it to me", he then went into the bedroom, picked Willy up and carried him to the boat, it was thick snow on the ground at the time, so imagine the strength of that man, to carry somebody down the 70 + steps to the quay, and put him on board.

Also Sandy had been drinking all day. Wow , but Willy told me that they caught a big trip, while he had a bigger hangover.

When Willy was young and on the deep water trawlers, he had an accident, and lost his thumb, the reason I am telling you this is that it has a lot to do with my last yarn.

When he was on the Congener with young Alan Morse, cook again, as they were steaming to the fishing grounds, Alan came into the mess deck, and started playing cards with the lads, now Alan was a BIG guy six foot six. While he was dealing the cards one of the lads commented on the size of his hands. Alan then said that you can tell the size of a mans penis by looking at the size of his thumb.

Willy went mad, and held his hand up. "are you trying to say that I haven't got a dick"?. Well the whole cabin cracked up.

THANK YOU. WILLY JACK.

THE END. PETER FRYER. LET GO

Peter Fryer went out on three fishing trips with the Bennison, a 60 foot anchor boat based in North Shields. It is skippered by Trevor Potter and his trusty crew; Davy, Taffy and Andy (Norman). Pete discovered early on that fishing is not some great romantic adventure. It is repetitive, dangerous and very often tedious.

As well as photographing the actual job of fishing, Pete Fryer was interested in the effects that the fishing process and the cramped living and working conditions has on the character of the crew. Each must find their own way of dealing with the potential claustrophobia and mental isolation. Emotions veer between extremes, from elation at a good catch to a plodding routine. Problems and mistakes have to be dealt with as they arise, sulking or hanging on to irritations can cause chaos. In some senses the skipper is isolated from the rest of the crew. It is accepted that he will make decisions for everyone about getting up at dawn; about working all the hours necessary; about how many hauls to do; about grabbing sleep when you can.

The romance of the job is in the strange relationship with the sea, its vastness its powers, its risk. Fishing is not only hard work, it is something beyond that, an obsession. Life outside work has to be squeezed into brief moments. Drinking acts as a buffer between one environment and the other. Problems with intimate relationships have to be piled into a few days, relationships with kids vie for the small space. Remembrance day is Thursday every week, when the wives go to collect their money. Remembering they have husbands.

Trevor J Potter

Ok lads where do we start fishing, I am getting a lot of crap on this.

Well pull in hope boys.

Fishing with the Ropes

Up anchor, and try again

Steaming to a new spot, it cannot be any worsera

Trevor J Potter

Well I am feeding someone.

At last a bit of life.

Fishing with the Ropes

Taffy notice the deck gear, while he is having a meal.

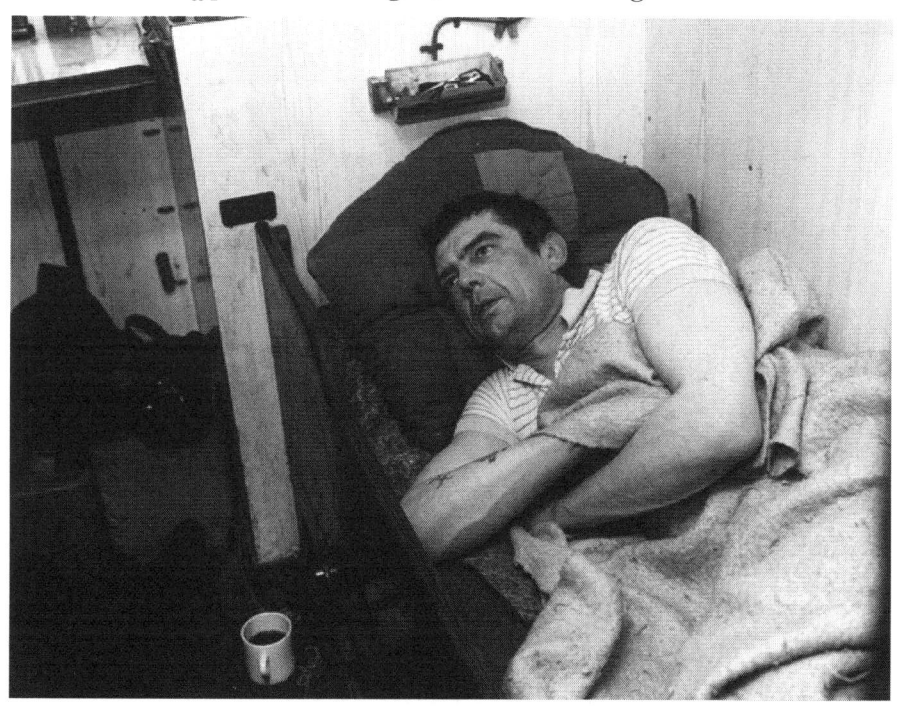

Trevor cannot sleep with the worry of no fish

Trevor J Potter

Andy the trainee cook, rolling tabs for the deck.

This is when I am not afraid to ask for advice.

Fishing with the Ropes

After a long night landing a bad trip.

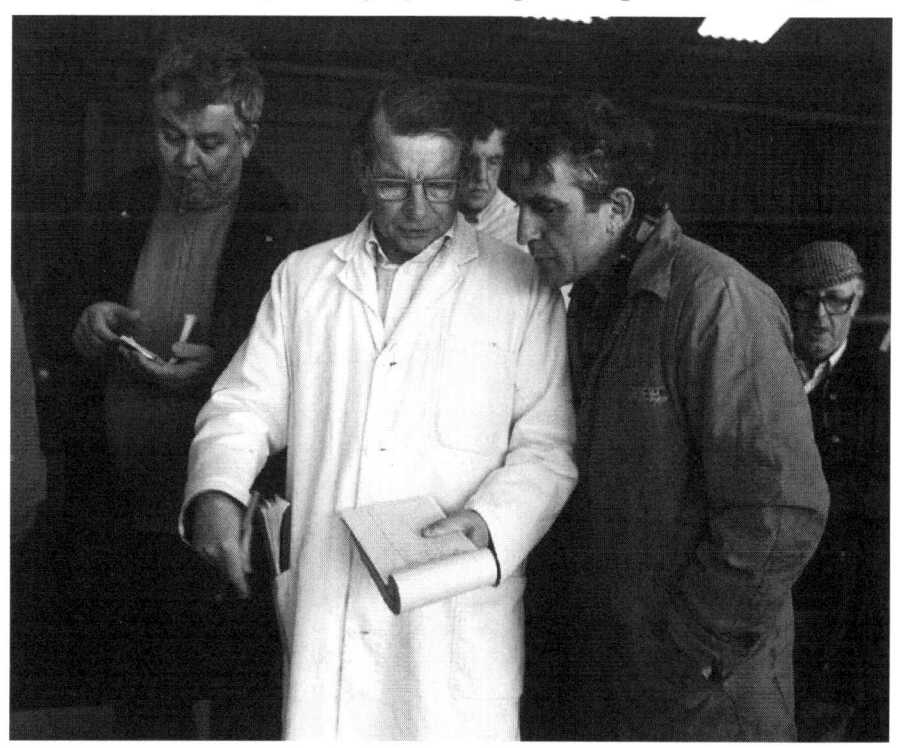

Davy checking the tally

Well mate better luck next trip?.

Well all I hope you enjoyed this book, and I hope I did not do your heads in, but like I said it was the book to break all the rules.

A book to let folks know about the ropes, and also the crap that the big trawlers gave to all the crews that stuck by them.

By all have a nice life, and if you have not read GRANDAD BOATS, Try it.

Thank you all Trevor James Potter.

I HAVE HAD SOME SAD NEWS THAT A CLOSE FRIEND HAS GONE TO FIDDELERS GREEN. R.I. P BAZ ROWLEY.

1960-2012.